Awakening to Living Energy

Merging the Human Presence
With the Cosmic Essence

by Beth L Robinson

DISCLAIMER:
The information within this book has been compiled by the author Beth L Robinson. While the opinions expressed herein are endorsed by the publisher, the publisher wishes to indemnify itself from any controversy that may arise as a result of misinterpretation or misunderstanding.

First Edition 2024
Copyright © 2024 by MetaVision Pty Ltd.
All rights reserved. The material contained within this book is protected by copyright law, no part may be copied, reproduced, presented, stored, communicated, or transmitted in any form by any means without prior written permission.

Artist – Princess Zebra (Front Cover – Art Work)

National Library of Australia
Cataloguing-in-Publication entry:

Awakening to Living Energy: Merging the Human presence with the Cosmic essence - Beth L Robinson.
Cosmic Awareness Series – Book Three: An historical recount of human development as advised by cosmic entity/energies.

1st ed.
ISBN 978-0-9580315-5-4 (pbk.).
ISBN 978-0-9580315-4-7 (epub.).

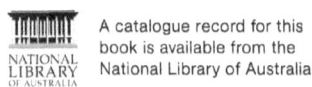

A catalogue record for this book is available from the National Library of Australia

Published by MetaVision Productions
Gold Coast Queensland, Australia.

Web Site: www.acosmicmind.com and www.divinewomanhood.com
Email: metavision37@gmail.com

TESTIMONIALS

Awe inspiring true storytelling at its finest! Thank you, Beth L Robinson for writing and sharing this life-changing book of greater understanding. I was touched deeply reading 'Awakening to Living Energy'. It was like sitting in front of a warm cosy fire, sipping my favourite wine. It drew me inwards. It was a very personal intimate experience as I explored and delved my way through like walking through a blooming garden of perfumed roses. Each paragraph and chapter was a sensory exploration of discovery and awareness, inner discussions and ponderings, tears, laughter, a melding, blending of mind and spirit.

The information and in depth explanations given of our forgotten human cosmic background are easily relatable and understandable through your talented recounting of human discovery and recovery. Thank you for sharing your gifted understandings for communal benefit.

Aria Kubach

****

A treasure trove of literary gems for those with an open and enquiring mind. An empowering read for all, but most importantly, to the awakened feminine mind. The important function of feminine energies and knowledge as Gaia evolves into the 5D, resonates deeply and supports my life calling, energy transmutation with frequency & sound.

Awakening to Living Energy is a bounty of ancient information, original poetry and the role of feminine power in the 5D futurity. A true example of Wisdom, Beauty, Style and Grace. Thank You Beth and cohorts for sharing this most valuable knowledge, confirming that Love is All.

Karen Betts - Energy Healer

****

I want to read more. The pearls of wisdom in this book are priceless! 'Awakening to Living Energy' had me enthralled throughout. My mind went into overdrive with the possibilities of the arrival of the New Day and the oncoming Fifth Dimension. Although I was aware of such huge shifts of the planet and the people, I had no idea there would be an awakening within myself of such brilliant proportions. The benefits of opening up from within as a blossoming flower held me in such awe that was compelling and overwhelming. My wish is to be more involved in the future Living Energy. Count me in!

Rebecca Hensher

****

A Cosmic Awakening

People on planet Earth
Wherever you come from
Whatever is stored within memory
Is part of a greater ME
You are a portion of eternal life
A written heritage in the stars
That is beyond mind and body

We are here to tell you clearly
Energy within soul cannot die
You may deny this message
You cannot deny your heritage
And most importantly
Connection with Great Mother energy

Dedication

Quote from Eastern mystic poet, Kabir

The flute of the infinite is played without ceasing and its sound is love. When love renounces all limits, it reaches truth. How widely the fragrance spreads. It has no ending; nothing stands in its way.

******

Our dedication and devotion, foremost, is to the Great Mother, the purveyor of female energy in the embrace of Love.

In our time spent in planetary notations and our background forming from cosmic fields, we wish to give due consideration to Angel energy. Angels on behalf of Mother Energy watch over us benignly. Angels have given us consideration for future benefit in acknowledgement of our dedication. They are our friends.

This We Pledge

We are aligned with those we cosmically represent

As devoted and dedicated children to the Great Mother, we are working in service to the Greater Energy. We have been nominated cosmically as lost children, yet with what we have come to understand in recent times, we consider we are no longer lost.

Who are we? That is the question each person is required to ask of the self. Given that we are prodigies of Greater Energy sent forth with roles to play out on this planetary orb called Earth is it necessary that we should know the answer to the question? Is the answer to the question simply to respond that we are in planetary appearance no one special. In effect we are projections of Greater Energy. We exist to use our planetary being for the benefit of developing a Greater Understanding of Love and Intelligence to be shared globally amongst tribal societies without discrimination.

In fact our cosmic roles on planet Earth are to ignite the energy fires of Love and Intelligence, which in turn will return missing elements of communal welfare into the arms and bosom of the Great Mother. Then in respect for her wisdom and beauty, we will involve and mentally embrace each other through absorbing the Greater Understanding incorporating Love energy. Thus far we are small in planetary numbers. However, our efforts in motivating human delivery into returning Home are designed to be witnessed as great. Our wishes in serving the Great Mother are beyond the wasted hopes of so many seeing themselves as superior in the operative planetary systems.

******

Our immediate purpose is to complete the elongated curve between Cosmos and planet Earth. This means that the journey already undertaken will complete through going full circle into establishing wholeness.

Our role on this planet today is mainly to ingest the minds of awakening people with the benefit of Greater Understanding in mind and memory. It is role-playing for us to divest others of what are wasted beliefs and then introduce new levels of Cosmic Intelligence. It is not our area to promote Love as such. Love energy will develop its own platforms for awakening the enclosed hearts. It will create its own level of fullness. We are not here to be seen as deliverers of Love, per se.

Our work is to step out momentarily from the absorption of Love Energy and by such means available introduce into people a Greater Understanding of Love. Though we can say we come from Love, which we do, it does not mean that we are to exude Love as such. For Love does not have need of proponents. Love exists within Love. Therefore, though we can say we are born of Love, which we are, we do not wish to demonstrate Love in planetary form or style.

What we can demonstrate are the areas that Love has decreed to be opened and developed; such as wisdom, beauty, and intelligence provisioning methods for Greater Understanding in mind. All of these agents are children of Love energy. Alternatively, if you prefer, they are an exponential evolvement of Love energy. As such, in obedience to the Great Mother whom we acknowledge as the female expansion of Love energy, we are her devoted children.

On a greater scale, some might say that is not exactly how life is to be seen, but we are not interested in working on that greater scale. What we are interested in doing is working within the arms of the Great Mother energy, so that the work we do on this planet echoes her brilliance, which is declared as wisdom, beauty, style, and grace.

So let us not get ourselves over excited about saying, 'oh, we can go back beyond that because we know that that was not the beginning'. Within our being we can have a small understanding of that, but if that is where we want to push a barrow then we will deny the area of work we have been put on this planet to develop. Therefore, we are all for obeying the wishes of the Great Mother.

Let others tell us that Love has its place and no doubt in their visionary platforms they see a greater picture developing. That is not our concern. We are not here to proclaim the be all and end all of human greatness, or of its intended cosmic fellowship.

We each have a role to play. We have beauty to observe within and then bring forth into light a display of its magnificence. We have a life to live and we have the concepts of Living Free to bring into prominence an effect that is still shrouded by a planetary dreaming state. That is an indication of our gifted roles; that is a small glimpse of our future work areas. In duty bound we will observe the necessary steps and so make the shifts in future happenings occur as smoothly as possible for advancing humankind.

****

Cover Explanation

The Sword in the Stone

The sword as illustrated is not an attack weapon. It is an emblem to signify that which is whole, what is worthy, a symbol representing unification of all being.

The stone represents the collective human brain. Two and a half million years ago when the sword was implanted into the stone representing human consciousness, it closed off the memory of human heritage and the connection to its cosmic family.

When the sword was driven into the capstone, it deprived humans of cosmic memory.

In November 1996, a small in numbers ceremony heralding the 11 11 gateway, participated in an awakening of long buried memories, where an enactment of roles were instituted through the ministration of Divine and Angel forces. The indicative sword of freewheeling energy was driven into the stone capsule of human enterprise and endeavour by Sataan at the behest of the Divine Mother. Thus it limited the capability of human memory to move past the conscious disarray that demonstrates discord. The sword was withdrawn from the capstone by Lucifer, the torchbearer of Intelligence, and returned to its cosmic sender post haste.

In the release caused from that action Intelligence is now free to advance from its unconscious format to replace the unwitting bondage of rational everyday mind and memory, which has been framed as a barrier to inner knowing by the repetitive use of patented planetary knowledge.

With the advent of Lucifer's arrival once more on the planet the institutionalised power framing of human control are doomed to crumble internally. The sun is rapidly setting on imperial influences of power and control that have held sway over people's thinking for far too long. The stamp of the alien superpowers is running dry of ink.

Websites and Internet exchanges will be the means of communication to correspond with those who welcome in A New Mind of intelligent persuasion and A New Day free of mental fear and painful pressure as illustrated by Covid 19 and subsequent viral strains.

Let the owners of modern day media outlets sink back into the turgid swampy hellholes of their own trivia style making. There will be no place available for their muckraking when the blue skies of the New Day over planet Earth open.

The Sword in the Stone was deliberately driven into mind and memory to keep the status quo as it was. The Mother veiled her face and she denied the exploitative entry into female worth, which is the only way to progress Love in being. You will not enter into Love until such times as you acknowledge the female worth or greatness in being. It is no good saying that you are female and so you have start in the game. You do not have start. You have no more start than the male counterparts do. The female worth that we speak of, which journeys into Love energy, is beyond the planetary ideas of female power.

An Explanation by Princess Zebra, the artist

The painting of the sword represents Truth in the hand of Lucifer, and the capstone represents the pain of blocked memory.

The Divine family sent me a vision:

- The four roses painted were representative of the four strands of colour of The Divine Mother, The Divine Father, Jesus and Lucifer.
- The vine surrounding it represents the Mothers.
- The hand of Lucifer with the sapphire ring is a signification of awakening and the awareness of taking the mantle of leadership.
- The diamond around the sword and the stone is the influence of Sataan.

After I finished the painting, the Strand of Energy came in to take us through a meditation called The Sword in the Stone. I invite you to go through the visualisation as you read it.

****

The Strand of Energy

11th July 2002

Cosmic Entity/Energy: Who wants the light of truth to shine upon you? Now you are in the light of sharing the light of truth. You may see it has an opening like a stream that has opened up for a greater communal benefit. Let us look at the stream. In the stream, we are seeing the purpose to be symbolic as a figure who is veiled. Entirely veiled.

There is an interchange of lightness and darkness, if you like. They are from the roots. It is dark and the head is light. Therefore, we can see this figure. It is approaching the stone of remembrance. The stone of remembrance is not of the memory banks that you have for planetary occurrences. It is, shall we say, your heritage and in the stone there is planted the sword of truth. The veiled figure approaches. Those of you who are ready can take the sword out of the stone with no obvious effort. It comes out easily for the veiled figure.

There is a streak of lightning flash and in the moment following that flash, Truth is merged back into the stream of living energy. So for each of you it can be opened up. In which case then you are able to move into the stream. To attempt to understand through rational thought will not get you linked with Truth. We are showing you in a symbolic manner what happens for the veiled figure. Perhaps you have figured it out for yourself. Not through rationalization of thinking. Truth will not be found there. Therein lie the lies abrogating worth and Beauty.

We hear what you say and we take little notice until the sword comes out of the stone. Until the veiled figure splits asunder. We thank you for your participation. We are merging back into the stream. You could see it as strands.

Luxor: Before you leave, can we ask how we identify you for posterity? Humans will want to know.

Energy: I work with the strands of Truth, Unity, and Equality and above all joy. Call me Strands of Energy, if you will.

Table of Contents

Introduction i
   A Cosmic Program i
Prologue iii
   A Tale of the Cosmic Wanderer iii
Chapter I   Cosmic Energy Within 1
   The Living Energy Within Being 1
   When First Awakened 2
   Lucifer speaks on Long Forgotten Understandings. 3
   Clearing the Mind 6
   Future of HU-man Kind 7
   Beliefs 9
   Hidden Realizations 11
Chapter II   Foundation Work 15
   Benchmark for Progression 15
   Collapsing Platforms of Beliefs 16
   Realising One Connective Energy 17
   What is Life? 18
   The Blue Print 21
Chapter III   Profiling 25
   Expanding the Bigger Picture 25
   Cosmic Pioneers of Futurity Benefit 26
   Cosmic Interlocutors 28
   Channelling 29
   A New Understanding 31
Chapter IV   The Product is You 37
   Cosmic Food on Offer 37
   The Emerging Product is Within You 40

    Innate Intelligence 41

    Explosion of Soul Energy 44

Chapter V   Promoting Personal Futurity 49

    The Birthing 49

    The Purpose of Future Human Growth 51

    Many Sizes in Personal Development 52

    Letting Go of Humanism 54

    Mind and Memory 55

    The Hard Yards in Building a Greater Understanding 57

Chapter VI   Greater Energy 61

    Love Absorbs All 61

    Discussion with the WE Energy 64

    We Who are Beyond Memory – Beyond the Human Idea 65

    The Unnamed Ones 65

    No Ritual 68

Chapter VII   New Millennium 69

    The False Dawn of 2000 69

    Interesting People 71

    2K Bug 73

    On Human Foundation 74

    The Future of Human Kind 75

    Spirituality and New Age 76

    Vitality and New Life 77

    The Kingdom of Heaven 78

    The End of a Period of Time 78

    Lucifer's take on New Age Hype 79

Chapter VIII   Legacy 81

    Futurity Benefit 81

Discussion with an Angel 81
Another Discussion with an Angel 84
Discussion with Beyond the Beyond 85
We Are One 88

Chapter IX   Self-Realizing.. 91
Unity and Being 91
Separation of Parts is Over 92
We are Nothingness 93
Building Harmonious Relationships 95
Lose the Outward Focus to Find the Internal Direction 95

Chapter X   The Living Energy... 101
Futurity exploration promotes one unified Self........................... 101
The Living Energy 102
Defining the Living Energy 104
Joy of Future Being... 105
The New Mind 106

Epilogue 111
Glossary 113
The Players accorded in the Divine Family Comedy 118
Greater Energy/Divine Plan and Greater Plan 120
About the Author 123
MetaVision Book Summaries 125
Book One — Gift of the Rose.. 125
Book Two — Awakening to a New Mind 127
Acknowledgements 129
Back Cover... 130

Table of Poems

A Cosmic Awakening 4

Our Tale of the Journey 12

Belonging 23

Uncompleted Rhapsody 34

Stand in Light 45

Many Books I have Read 59

The Embrace of the Beloved Mother – Oneness 67

A Moving Day Expanding Love 80

Notation from the Angels 90

Understanding the All 100

Living Channels of Energy 110

Introduction

A Cosmic Program

This is a compendium of essays illustrating *Awakening to Living Energy, merging the essence maintained within with the human presence without.*

A Cosmic Program equals a Greater Understanding of who you truly are. Some of the language used will be unfamiliar to some so a Glossary has been provided at the end of the book.

Some people may think that what we offer gladly for mental consummation will lessen their participation in planetary living. What is on offer is an expansion of Life and Living Free arrangements within being as we enter the Fifth Dimension. Present day living standards in society are to be rearranged without the mock clemency of paternal coverage on display as it is today.

As an introduction to the essays illustrating the Greater Understanding within, let us affirm there is Angel energy involved in plotting human advancement in mind and memory. Our essays are notated from various cosmic entity/energies, so there is more than one viewpoint being displayed. Expect some overlapping with the essays and discussions. Each relate to a version that will suit the taste buds of some. There are no hard and fast rules.

We are designated cosmic stargazers intent on sharing the visions of human advancement referenced as back to a future that is waiting to be realized. We consider there will soon arrive for human deliberation a Fifth Dimensional influence of cosmic persuasion signifying a uniformity of racial differences and equality of persons. Futurity living arrangements are not out there. Understandings maintaining the required balance and direction to guide your steps in life are within you.

As Jésu said many years ago, 'eventually each of us has to come to understand that the struggle for purposeful delivery is never out there'. The coming to terms of balanced arrangement has to be played out within ourselves. When you are prepared to admit that, when you are prepared to acknowledge there is no person, no thing, no situation outside of you that is hampering or badgering your progression. What is delaying your future development of worth is seated inside your framing of memory.

Awakening to Living Energy

Prologue

A Tale of the Cosmic Wanderer

One evening as the stars came into play with no promise of moonlight the cosmic wanderer came to the door of an isolated house, drawn there by a soft light reflected in the window. He knocked gently on the door and when the occupant appeared, he requested entry as the darkening night showed certain signs of inclement weather. He offered an exchange of experiences in reciprocation for the kindness of shelter.

The dweller welcomed him in because news of the outside world was infrequent and he relied on visitors for information. He seated the wanderer in the kitchen and offered food that he heated on a wood-burning stove. A lantern hanging from an overhead beam dimly lighted the room.

The wanderer glanced around and saw that the room was stocked with electrical equipment. 'Why do you prefer secondary power when electricity is available' he questioned. The dweller acknowledged his lack of understanding of electricity. He was employed to house sit and he awaited the return of the owners. The wanderer located the power entry box and threw the switch that lit the different rooms.

In the morning he spent some time explaining the use of different facilities to the astonished dweller who kept repeating to himself that he would never have believed it if he had not been shown first hand. Then they sat down and the wanderer spoke to him of life.

He emphasized the importance of love and joy that comes with understanding the experiences drawn from the many probabilities of people he encountered in the variegated pathways of life journeying. The dweller asked the wanderer where he had gained his initial understanding and what universities of knowledge had he attended.

The wanderer laughed in delight at the questioning and answered by saying it was a gift of lighted energy he carried within, which had become ignited through cosmic agreement. 'Everyone carries the internal gift like a rosebud waiting for its moment of abundant expression. Very few are aware of what they carry in inherent memory because, perversely, they refuse to look within their being. They insist that what appears to be 'out there' should be satisfying

Awakening to Living Energy

to the focus of their eyes. When they learn to turn their heads and realign their vision the gift of life is then revealed.'

The dweller though perplexed by what seemed an insurmountable fount of information could feel a stirring begin somewhere within his very being. A desire borne from memory pierced his mind and shook his frame and he felt hot tears spring to his eyes. Suddenly he had a yearning for a return to a home of belonging although he could not name the place. His mind framed a question that came from somewhere deep within. 'How will I come to know my gift?'

The wanderer's reply came easy and reassuring. 'Open your arms to Love without any consideration of advantage and the connection will be made.' He prepared himself to leave but the dweller held his arm. 'Who are you and what is your purpose in travelling?'

Again, the wanderer laughed and the sounds of spontaneity in mirthful rapture rippled through the room like spring water splashing down over outcrops of barren rocks.

'I am known as The Unnamed One who is elected to carry abroad the torch of Intelligence. The purpose can be seen as a heralding of light that shineth brightly to dispel shadows of darkness. It comes into fruition as surely as the New Day is upon us. Where I walk the brush-fires of pain and fear are exposed and then extinguished to make way for the roses of Love to bloom'.

Then the Cosmic Traveller was gone yet the warmth he spread still lingered and the dweller went into a state of instant reverie. When he awoke from the dream state he found that both his arms and his mind were opened in acceptance.

Written by Lucifer

Chapter I

Cosmic Energy Within

The Unnamed One: *Futurity living arrangements are not out there. Understandings maintaining the required balance and direction to guide your steps in life are within you.*

The Living Energy Within Being

The Living Energy within is the core of being. The Angels also reference the core as Home. Destiny, which we call futurity, is homeward bound. Home is within the memory of being. Remember the childhood games where home was the achievable goal.

As we move into the Fifth Dimension, the explosion of soul energy in line with The Living Energy and Awakening to A New Mind is being matched by soul energy becoming more vital and apparent. The merging of essence and presence is to be registered in a form of mental agreement.

The present day human system is disparately scattered and lacking conformation. Human mental systems are isolated and separated. The vocal entity is presence and the silent energy of stillness in soul is essence. The disparate portions, we describe as scattered pieces, are to be joined in mutuality.

Cosmic programming promotes a Greater Understanding of who you truly are designated to realize as being whole.

There is a cosmic program of treasured futurity nestled deep inside each of us. It is accessible in mind and memory when we step away from our present day planetary rooted systems of belief and denial.

Awakening to Living Energy

Learn to know instinctively there is a cosmic program of futurity worth securely hidden within each psyche collection of memories. Through a small series of staged sessions indicated for discussion purposes, a cosmic program will be revealed with the recovery of unified self through mentally retracing your antecedent steps: understanding that which you truly are in spirit, as well as the discovery of a greater wealth of understanding is already waiting to be revealed within each wakened being.

Until we are able to broach nothingness by shutting down extraneous type thinking completely, the distant memories of cosmic journeying are not available for conjecture.

Love energy absorbs those who wait with open arms. Cosmic intelligence infiltrates the minds of those prepared to acknowledge a defining doorway to destiny. The Greater Understanding is like a fine mist of advanced benefits you are to welcome into your system. You are wet thoroughly when you accept the cosmic programming enjoining your forecast level of consciousness.

Future living arrangements in mind and memory are not out there for random choosing.

Greater Understandings maintaining the required balance and direction to guide your steps through life are stored within you. The human system is similar to a budding flower; it blossoms from the inside out. So copying other people with their whims and fancies may appear as a glamorous pursuit of idle fancy, but it does not fulfil the requirement of wholeness resolutely determined within.

Let us suggest that within each persona there is a resident self, waiting to come forward and greet our present being with a harmonious embrace, which like the petals of the Rose will open a new vista of meaningful purpose into present day living standards. Prepare to engage with a Personal Futurity and enjoy the awakening thrill of a stirring strangeness vibrating within your very being.

****

When First Awakened

The New Day is dawning clear. New Life means new purpose in mind and memory development.

Lucifer: Education is a wonderful thing, though it cannot possibly develop without first having a basic understanding of words rooted in Intelligence.

With that in mind, each of us has to consider going back in memory to an academic school of cosmic learning. It is an Acadème of involved study in the very beginning of conscious awareness, which is called cosmic birthing.

Who amongst all of us is capable of moving back to where we first became awakened? You may think that your awareness of conscious thinking on planet Earth is where you began, or even your awareness or awakening within a particular star system is where you should begin. No one can possibly establish where they initially began emerging because there was no beginning.

Question: Are you saying it is possible to go back beyond your birth date?

Lucifer: Yes. It is a very simplistic word. It is called nothingness. Science knows of its vastness, but because they cannot measure it, they will not give it precedence. Metaphysical studies know of it, but they will not give it precedence. Religions are aware of its magnificence. They will not give it precedence.

Out of a void of nothingness emanated everything imaginable in mind. The most beautiful energy that you will ever have the opportunity of enjoining is in the realization that you are in effect a product of nothing comprehensible. It is from that state of hidden awareness you are given the mental tools to create new patterns of Greater Understanding.

****

Lucifer speaks on Long Forgotten Understandings.

The cosmic understandings that we offer for consideration do not stem from temporal beliefs. They are maintained by an acceptance of energies far larger in scope and magnificence than the rational minds of ordinary humans have any possibility of grasping. Cosmic Ancients and Angels are our tertiary tutors and instructors. Their vital energy comes from beyond the cosmic planes, their fields of terrestrial work. We work by agreement on their behalf throughout the Cosmos.

Two and a half million years ago as cosmic pioneers, nominated as the 37, we came to planet Earth and we stood the species of humanoids called man on their feet. We have returned many times since to assist humankind reach and adapt to new levels of self-discovery. This time we act as instruments that assist in reconnecting planet Earth and its occupants back to the cosmic levels from where its planetary futurity first commenced. We call it going Home. It has also been expressed poetically by some as returning 'back to the future'.

Awakening to Living Energy

The comprehensive fixtures of rational/logical mind settings have been built from platforms of ideals drawn from repetitive material called knowledge. The tarted up inspirational thoughts of the present day are rehashed versions of old ideas. They come bubbling to the mental surface from stagnant pools of distant memories. The rational memory banks of psyche feed recorded messages that reaffirm rationality, which has been built from resolving past insecurities. The platforms of insecurity promote fear, resulting in those relying on old habits to seek security. Which social system can claim it is clear of planetary pain and beyond the dread of fearing unknown causes? Fear is a knotted whip for people lacking in understanding to mentally assail themselves.

It is a method of primitive development that having erupted through pain, continuously encountering aberrant pressure valves from fixed lines in memory to recycle once more and appear in some other sense or manner. This initially may appear as a glamorous fare yet cannot sustain or fulfil the need and greed inherent in the human system. Satisfaction in the misguided mind and memory is momentary pleasure only. Why should this be so or allowed to remain?

The simple explanation for this is because the rational/logical minds have developed from past insecurities and so the cycle is required to return to clear the fear base that is painfully caught in DNA memory. That the rational mind is both erotic and neurotic is not obvious at first glance, because the early neuroses are shared with groups of others; this does not allow the singular mind the opportunity to establish reference points within the framing of each nominated picture.

Can the donkey reach the carrot of desirability through exerting extra effort? It cannot. Yet the fixated desires or urges that the human minds contain drives and compels people to strive for what are unattainable positions, or situations, which prove on further discovery to be untenable.

What is deemed unattainable? The idealistic dreams that have been cleverly planted within the mental systems to control waywardness in humanity. There is a vexed desire for obtaining immortal recognition. We call this aborted craving the god system. The god system has been built without substantial supporting features and retains little or no authority. It is maintained through the promise of punishment and reward. Of necessity the punishment or abuses in living practices come first.

Then the anticipated promises of just rewards will be fulfilled later. Or will they?

Can people see that they are conditioned to beat themselves up repeatedly for the immortal promise of just rewards? What do they see as their planetary rewards? An ownership on thwarted values called choice and freewill. Ownership is listed under the law of diminishing returns. The more effort you put in, the less you will eventually draw out. Does more effort return more rewards? Can rewards by being multiplied in number maintain greater levels of satisfaction?

Multiplied rewards offer compensations of material benefits. The compensations are required substitutes for the lack of emotional balancing. Who is emotionally balanced when chasing after monetary dreams of wealth? Are the tycoons fixated on making piles of money in a state of relaxation or are they driven by mental demons, which suggest that bigger returns have to be better and brighter in value?

When the acquisitive mind seeking for what is not readily available switches on who can turn it off? Can empire building produce the joy in satisfaction and then sustain it? For humans joy appears to be like a shadow that moves within a dreaming state. Dreaming does not carry lasting joy. At most it carries illusionary visions of momentary splendour. When will the dreamers on planet Earth awaken from their slumber? Soon. Very soon.

The New Day will be brought into being bearing the light of two sons on behalf of The Divine Mother energy. The cosmic self to be awakened is situated inside each one of us. The unified connection can be made through balancing the two energies, presence and essence, contained within each system. The varied imbalances are required to be dissolved through the equation of differences. Some people mistakenly call them opposites.

Nobody can sell you joy that sustains your being. That joy is elusively maintained within the internal you. It is dormant, an untapped energy on hold. We can offer you cosmic information that will allow you to awaken and access your own feelings of joyful participation. Humans have sold themselves short by the expectations of receiving benefits from other sources to fulfil their long forgotten dreams.

Invest some small effort in locating your innate self. The returns are guaranteed. The daily profit margins exceed anything that stock markets can offer. Their offerings are never more than temporary gains. The eternal energy, which dwells within all beings, when awakened offers a new Life and Living free arrangement.

****

Clearing the Mind

Clearing the mind of detrimental garbage we nominate as baggage may seem like a painstaking workload. For those who have the courage to stay committed to the coalface it can at times appear arduous. Just keep chewing away one bite at a time to clear the mind of detritus. It is similar to dieting. The secret to achieving success is in eating less, more often.

The ego system you have been trained to denote as self-esteem is an overlay of who you are. The persona you work with daily is no longer effective for future development on the planet. When are you prepared to break down this persona of self that you have been overlaid with by goodwill people, those who thought they were working in your best interests? When you are able to let that mirrored imagery go or break it apart, when you have located those who you truly represent, then you can build a fresh personal being of individual strength in character.

More specifically open your arms and agree to wear the personal built individual styling for you to develop cosmically, which will allow you to interact with people on the planet where you are going to be able to provide the most communal benefit. The benefit of Love energy flows in many ways. First, it is to flow through your internal system and then it can on flow to benefit others.

When you cease seeking answers from outside sources is the day you will find within who you are designated to reveal. That is why we advocate sitting still and silently opening your arms to receive direction. It is known cosmically as surrendering to a greater unnamed energy.

Solidify that which is within and the without proceedings will fall into place. Ground your own area of mental stability and what there is surrounding you will make sense. First, realize sensibility is nurtured from within. Humans are taught to focus too much attention on the outer scenarios and do not look inwards for understanding there is a bigger picture evolving.

The Greater Energy calls the shots on futurity measures, but it has been revealed to us that they cannot fire the enthusiasm of any human interest intent on downward spiralling. The purposeful deeds of mental discovery and recovery of cosmic memory are to be performed on a planetary level. To inspire the coded enthusiasm in others demonstrate a willingness to rearrange mental patterns within that are caught in dire straits of discord.

While people disrespect their inner being, they cannot help but dislike and mistrust the actions of others. Thus, the research for developing Greater

Understanding has to start within being. People are to realize that the rewards of Living Free of detrimental damage are inside each of us. Until they can grasp that level of Greater Understanding, they are condemned to continue living the planetary dreams that mislead mental enthusiasm for glamorous pursuits leading to nowhere.

****

Future of HU-man Kind

People on planet Earth live a narrowed and focused existence, because being cast in singular fashion; they cannot mentally gain access to examine the surrounding areas of a bigger cosmic picture. Most people exist in a world of shadowed imagery because they have not learnt to engage and embrace the brighter lights of Greater Understanding.

Dreams of future growth are patterned thoughts, still housed in their boxed areas of limitations. The futurity of human growth rests within the extended harmony shared between ordinary people. First, they are to learn to build a range of productive elements contained within their selves.

Your future companion, partner or co-worker who is presently missing may walk into your life at any time. How would you recognize them instantly if you do not have a clear understanding of who you are? This world is full of Cinderellas who, without the use of a reflective mirror, think their present persona guise is attractive to inveigle an unwary Prince Charming. How many princesses would be turned on by a male companion appearing in their life in the guise of a grubby chimney sweep? Should women work at awakening from their dreaming or dream on while working as some frowzy typecast Cinderella?

Successful lives are built on firm foundations of worthwhile substance. Should the visual surface state of glamorous appeal get a serious look in?

****

We have been asked by cosmic Angels to write on their behalf certain understandings of where humanity stands locked in thrall today, how life came to be where it is presently situated, and where the future of humanity is heading apace. This exchange deals very much with basic practicalities and probabilities of future global events.

Awakening to Living Energy

The related stories deliver anecdotal material very much like a primary reader for small children; they have a vague awareness of their surroundings without the expansive background of Greater Understanding. When we have the opportunity to discuss the issues and destiny of future life, planet Earth and its creatures, we have gifted the realization that, beyond the delivery of scholarly knowledge for human consumption there are due to surface deeper strains of Greater Understanding carrying many unrealized benefits.

Through an overload of scattered beliefs, the everyday mind maintains a series of mental fetters echoing from inglorious past events. These manifest into control patterns that do not necessarily lead to releasing pain from atmospheric pressure.

'Why transfer to us the job of wakening the minds of people?' was the responsive denial we muttered for a number of years. In the early stages, the Angel response was a brief 'Why not indeed?' Now that our understandings have been broadened through cosmic style forms of advanced education, we are more comfortable with the tasking roles we are set to rearrange.

The given cosmic understandings we receive are not linked with planetary style patterns of belief. That which is relayed cosmic information is maintained by an acceptance of the wisdom of entity/energies ranging far larger in scope and magnificence than the rational mind of the human presence has any possibility of grasping.

This does not mean we consider that human minds through receiving a conveyed cosmic message cannot grasp its portent. However, cosmic understandings exceed the capacity of limited rational thought, where ideas of planetary existence have been built from superstitious platforms of religious and scientific beliefs. The years of sustained mental pressure, which people endure endlessly on this planet fade into insignificance when people are made aware of the futurity roles determined for advancing humankind.

Controlling factors, dramas, traumas, warfare, and separations, are some of the nightmare elements that precede the New Mind awakening to the dawning of a New Day. People are experiencing the closing down of a millennium, an unstable era, yet even more importantly, it is a closing of the last chapter of this third dimensional stage in the book of cosmic life. People are weathering a stormy final chapter in a global series that has lasted 2,500,000 years in linear time.

Beliefs

As we have stated previously these essays are not meant to endorse a book about some newfound beliefs that attract virtual excitement. We would rather people allowed their minds to stay open and let resonate within their systems that which is meant to vibrate and circulate new material. The rational or so-called logical mind fastens onto beliefs like oyster shells attach to rock faces, which tends to make sure that planetary mindsets remain concreted in suspect dreams of quantified reality.

A belief is like a floating airborne balloon without a fixed foundation. What we are saying is that if a belief was capable of grounding it would rearrange in living energy to be shown as a knowing.

So do we have a belief in Angels? Not a belief, for Angel energy is acceptable to those who are able to work with other galactic levels or dimensions of existence. The beings of light, those that speak mentally through us have the physical use of a medium's vocal chords when necessary. This arrangement is performed by cosmic agreement. An agreement, we are told, that was made aeons ago.

To awaken consciously is an opportunity to reclaim some of our lost memories. When we are aware of who we truly are, there is no longer a need for seeking ego frames of protection. No one needs to be saved. Those who tell you Jesus appeared as a saviour on the planet are confused by their own muddled, wishful type of religious thinking.

Fear is a weapon of choice with which people assail their selves first and then deliver onto others. Life has many illusionary features demonstrating planetary happenings of then and now yet there is a new life beckoning beyond the restrictions of conditioned thinking. If such were not so, living energy would not be deemed eternal. When we seek the rose, we grasp the thorn of mental disclosure and some mistake as reality the respondent pain for what is registered.

Let us say to those who have advanced enough in understanding to see death forms as a release, a letting go of planetary circumstance. Were you to let go of convoluted issues before you physically die, death becomes meaningless. Were we to step through a darkened doorway into another lighted room, do we bemoan the loss of movement from one space into another? Who gave death the elevated position it now occupies in religiously based society rituals? What keeps hope relevant in doubtful minds except the superstitions of those who preach protection from harm?

Awakening to Living Energy

The human is a semi-programmed creature working through a procession of realization, which is called life. Shakespearean sonnets humorously noted seven stages.

Premise, which is at the base of suggested knowledge, has as much stability as the drift of tidal sand. Knowledge, or that portion people accept as valid in learning skills, has its use by date approaching. Adapted to suit the occasion, altered to appease the contrary whims of a captive audience, evolution is a continuing process of breaking down old patterns so new forms of Living Energy have the opportunity to emerge and engage. Emerging is the operative word, for just like the growth of small children, people require new things to replace old habitual things. Just as items of clothing are dated, the human child of whatever age is destined to grow out of this and into that.

The growth is life, demonstrating flux and flex, tooing and froing, pushing and pulling into new arrangements. There is a constant rhythm within the internal system, a hum of cosmic energy, an atonement of selves reaching out to meld and merge in agreement.

One exception to the gentle flow of energy we call Living Free is the diverse machinations of the chattering and scolding human mind that is ego driven. For some reason the mechanized cogs in the brain are always getting stuck. The mind appears to hold a fascination to possess objectivity as an ownership of other things. It is in this claim of ownership that the needle for future growth tends to stick. Insecure people, in the craving urge to amass physical possessions, causes any number of perverse imbalances that upset the coordinated balance in mutual relationships.

The desire to be seen as someone of importance takes precedence over the opportunity to relax and allow life to give us what is available for amicable enjoyment. Inspired by greed people are too busy taking away from others property rights they do not need to acquire. Like ants, sensing a big wet season ahead, those who are mentally deprived or depraved, have the urgency to accumulate more and more wasteful possessions, bred into their systems by the lingering meanness in society values.

In an attempt to grow and expand, people can no more help the changes they cause than the physical body can deny the onset of puberty. Humans are creatures of destiny, playing out life, piece by piece, with those who invented the gaming of ownership. When will humans concede the learning table labelled as knowledge is in a state of suspension and realize it is time to selectively move forward to embrace new forms of advanced intelligence?

As a formulated species, people have become fixated with a large number of mythological mistakes. A major one is that they are moulded into a superior form of uniqueness, given the right to control, molest and abuse other forms of life if the idea is deemed profitable or seen as appealing.

People have been sold the idea that there is such a thing as body perfection or, as Plato would have put it, an ideal worthy of grasping. This ideal of perfection presumably will lead them out of the tangled wilderness of errant thoughts retained in psyche and give to the true believers their rightful share of a promised land called heaven.

Are you getting the sinking sensation that the rhythmic needle is stuck in a planetary crack once more? Which countries in the world have created a meaningful balance between different races of people and the environment of nature so that those affected by mental unease and disease can readjust and learn to live in states of harmonious relationships?

Hidden Realizations

We offer a product of Intelligence that expands human understanding beyond the planetary discourse of knowledge. We first must acknowledge we are amateurs or mavericks in pioneering this particular field of Genius Style Living. As such, we are guided by greater cosmic energies.

In outlining the story of developing humankind, understand that it promotes a realization of hidden energy enclosed within the depths of being. *Being* is like a secret key because it denotes cosmic strains of energy that are locked within each planetary system. Humans are trained from childhood to look outwards for plausible answers or excuses while the absolving of problematic questioning is enclosed within. Realization defines early measures of Greater Understanding. Realization carries a far deeper meaning in responsible human development than planetary areas of conditioning.

Human memories fall short of decisive conclusions. People do not finish sentences. Therefore, they are mentally in debt or still caught in a mental system that indicates various forms of slavery. How many people give humans their correct title adjudged as human being? Humankind references planetary style living derangement and being is cosmic related. *Being* is the operative word describing the involvement of presence and essence; like being in the bigger picture.

Human systems of today are living on borrowed time. This means they have built up a debt that has not been paid in full and therefore has to be serviced regularly or annulled.

****

Our Tale of the Journey

We come and our tale of the journey
Amongst preset lifestyles of the many
Are as vanishing footfalls in memory
Washed clean in the care of Mother Sea

Until one day people will lift their gaze
To mountaintop through mist and haze
Above which shines a luminous star
A burning cross symbolled from afar

Then the minds of many will be at a loss
To distinguish a star from the fiery cross
Call of memory scented from the Mother
Each traveller awakens to greet another

Where forms the thirst, the grail, the word
A destined stone waits with shining sword
The Prince of Darkness joyously unguards
Endorsing old friends walking extra yards

Flash of fairy light colours a shining way
Elfin help gifted by Merlin, some say
Held aloft is the promise of eternal life
A flaming torch disperses miasmic strife

A bended knee doth complete the tasking
Without any spurious claims or plea
A simple response to the Mother asking
Will you as my children die for ME

Awakening to Living Energy

Chapter II

Foundation Work

The Unnamed One: *You will all come to realize that when you bare your soul no one has a problem or issue with you. It is the covering of denial that brings on the virtual attackers.*

Benchmark for Progression

The modern mind raised in childhood while adapting to society values does not have a benchmark to maintain the essential balancing in mind, neither within nor without.

Why is it so important that in these harrowing times ahead for civilization we are required to locate foundation in mind and memory, the very basic groundwork of being? Only then, we can build into unifying effect the new mind stemming from the roots of cosmic foundation. The Angels have suggested we first work to find the benchmark for progression within our distant memory cells.

To embrace the state of nothingness, which clears the mind and brain of superfluous junk material is the recommended benchmark to establish a grounded area in being. Realize that one by one equals one. It smashes open the locks of presumed duality in choice and freewill. With the collapse of duality that which will be demonstrated for the purposeful achieving Greater Understanding are the principles of Truth, Unity and Equality.

Can you agree we are required to first fall out of balance to readjust and find the innate core of a balanced reserve? If we want the true starting line then we are to go beyond egoistic practices and locate our core of inner self to establish the relative survey peg or benchmark. There is the starting line of atonement awakening each presence to a New Mind delivery and the essence of Living Energy programmed within.

We are to lose all proprietary thoughts of greed and thus find the energy of Love within or is it when neediness in greed is erased, Love then embraces us? The realization that the foundation of all life is LOVE will become established as the benchmark for appropriate proceedings in futurity relationships.

We are to align with the infrastructure of the Diamond essence. The Diamond Effect is an energy field that is still in the process of unfolding. (We will uncover more understanding in Book IV of our series.) To complete our designated work areas, this unfolding agenda of our exploration, the memory of who we are, the wholeness in being with the inner benefits it promotes, must remain as a constant benchmark.

****

Collapsing Platforms of Beliefs

Areas of work procedure and simplistic methods to find new ways of achieving competency are available on request.

A mental platform of beliefs when it disintegrates requires somewhere else for our mental systems to move into new activities; otherwise, we will sink with the collapsing platforms of ego pretence.

When we rebuild our internal house within from a firm foundation, we can then collapse the framed surrounds of immature ego scaffolding. Mentally we can move within to locate the foundation or core in being that is not dependent on planetary self-esteem, which relies on ego fads of selfishness for society type management roles.

The core self within is the foundation of being. How do we locate or touch base with the integral core? First, let go of an egoistic self-pretence and thus remove the protective coating of a wilfully charged persona attitude. What can we do to willingly further the benefit of Mother Energy today? Acknowledge there is a bigger picture in life waiting to unfold its futurity benefits when engaging in communal practices.

Give to people brief explanations on Fifth Dimensional advancement in mental growth that invite open-ended responses. What is meant by furthering Intelligence growth when viewed on a planetary level? Can it be there is a latent projection of Greater Understanding awaiting discovery from hidden memory banks in psyche?

Regardless of how much knowledge is absorbed and applied via formal education in this panicked world of warring and bickering slander today, the vast majority of people remain inducted in singular habits where only 50% of any living picture is made visible or viable for comprehensive study. In the dimly lit scenarios of changing world patterning, the present end times are quite often viewed as gloomy and tough.

The emotional demands being made on the timelines of professional support systems become ever-increasing burdens. The quota of available intelligence entering the labour market is strained and stretched tighter than many people would like to think is possible to endure.

Now is the hour to lighten up the mental load through understanding the principles that formulate standards of Living Free arrangement. A New Mind is attainable through embracing greater levels of brain development emanating from advanced degrees of cosmic Intelligence.

****

Realising One Connective Energy

We are meant to meld body, mind, brain and spirit into a unified and equalized substantial energy. This will demonstrate Truth according to their planetary tastes without the frills and fanciful touches that adorn religious faith and scientific attempts to harness a spiritual denial. We intend firstly, to share the realization of Living Free of crass impediments to confound and then astound any sceptical audience under the title of 'Merging Three Aspects of living component energy into one unified benefit', which signifies the element of wholeness in mandated being.

People may wonder how we can manage to work a human mind and body system into effectively sharing a mutual enclave with spirit energy. The simple response is that cosmic based energy formulated into planetary beings can work its way Home by combining a diversity of styles or fashion. The key to clearing away puzzlement in mind is to strip the façade of planetary thinking held in a third dimensional vacuum that denies the awakening of fresh growth in the essence of soul. So let go of an ego plastered god sense maintaining wasted beliefs as well as the descriptive phrasing of erroneous ideas about gaining an ascendancy of spiritual uplifting.

Simplicity is the key to converting three disparate segments into one connective energy. Acknowledge there are presently voided gaps of separation maintained between body, mind and spirit. Allow for a small margin of differences. The body will usually follow the direction of mind so we can allow that procedure to continue. Spirit energy will no longer sit back. We are to work at rejoining spirit with the ego spaced mental aperture sometimes referenced as 'you,' as in the Angel questioning, 'who are you?'

Where do we begin to reunite portions of a fragmented past into a mutuality of togetherness? First, we are to strip the dried out leaves of faded belief surrounding the flowering essence instead of attempting to gild the fronds of a faded lily. In other words we are to remove extraneous material cluttering the mind that is no longer purposeful.

Emphasis needs to be taken off the tarted image of body beautiful. Let go of idealistic typeface sculpture, tattoos, fat shaming, and gym workouts designed to promote the body shape of mean, lean, hungry and unfortunately angry personas.

****

What is Life?

It has been stated generally that very rich people only make pretence of having big hearts and have even deeper pockets.

What is life is a question aimed at broadening the minds of enquiring humans beyond the limited capacity derangement obtained from the curriculum of patented knowledge. We offer cosmic based information that will rearrange set patterns in the mind and realign its purposeful direction to connect with beyond cosmic Intelligence. Extraneous to the magnetic pull of third dimensional space, which is contained within the atmospheric pressure surrounding Earth, are many advanced life forms. Some of these carry similar interests and others offer further benefits for human development by sharing information through the connective energy of Greater Understanding.

Whatever has a formative setting in planetary mind framing in some way references a thing. Everything known and named on the planet is a manifested projection forming from an expressive image abstracted cosmically and implanted into a third dimensional state of cognisance. Recognition for the human senses is then instigated from these memory patterns of consciousness operative within localised brain cells.

Within the human system of structured body and mind, there are many operative life patterns. Each living thing breathes energy from Life and carries

Foundation Work

a spark of light evident in the eye, which draws material to the conscious surface level from deep wells of intelligent memory. The harboured spark of cosmic light is not accessible to the measuring gauges of science because it operates within an internal system and is thus beyond the capability range of third dimensional instruments. If the rationale of modern scientific studies still says that only things observable are to be validated then their aim is to confine the thought forms of lesser people to be used mainly as an advantage for their particular persona selves.

Forms are relative to the particular area of use. In third dimensional terms human form and matter is acknowledged as physical and materialistic. Because of its lowered level into third dimensional density that causes a shadow to be cast when making contact with light energy. Within the mental systems relaying DNA strands from memory there are also shadows of resistance carrying onward the painful pressure of unresolved issues from past happenings.

The soul energy is hidden in its expression; in scientific terms it has not been generally seen as a contributing factor involved in daily experience. This contentious situation is about to be rearranged by cosmic intervention. The time is nigh for the development of the soul entity to move from a transparency stage into an apparent or recognisable state of cosmic consciousness. That might be seen by science as a form of evolvement though more accurately because of impression it will paradoxically be expressed as involvement rather than just material alignment. Scientific quote: it only exists because you can kick it. Alternatively, should that situation be read in reverse? 'I think, therefore, I am' of Descartes' note is questionable.

What is Life? At present on the planet, it can only be recognizable in a narrowed proportional sense of birthing, living and dying. The understanding of Greater Energy and entities ineffable and indistinguishable in human terms has defied accurate or adequate description for eons. Any relating of experiences beyond empirical measurement is subjected to ridicule by arrogant people fearful of what today or tomorrow may bring because of persistent enquiry. You can include those whose minds are prone to be sceptical because of their own ineptitude steeped in stains of ignorance, arrogance and superiority type judgement.

We say all Life is an energy distribution coming from the foundation of Love. It is observable in the spark that leaps into flame in the eyes of the newborn. It is available to be identified in the sensory touch of the elasticity of skin enclosing the breathing body. It moves away with the leaving of energy that sustained the breath in physical form. Eternal energy that feeds the renewal of life cannot die though it constantly works in various stages or degrees of rearrangement.

It has been said that bodies formed from the dust of earth are subject to linear time, therefore in death they succumb to nature and lapse back into planetary origins called organisms. The energy assigned to the soul with its inbuilt memory of psyche does not die because its inner strength of light energy is unattached to planetary conditioning.

When seated in a vehicle does that make you a part of the carriage mechanism? Being encased in a body form, does that make your brain system subject to the whims of body expression or determination? It is, only if you are inclined to believe it to be so. Being introduced into mind, can thoughts of immortality build the steps necessary to sustain life by constantly affirming erroneous patterns of beliefs? Being clothed in religious habit, will spiritual notions of an almighty god sense find for true believers a feather bed in a nominated hereafter state called heaven above?

Do the pundits proclaiming science, being universally skilled, that is historically, ritually, and traditionally favoured in their trained mannerisms of research, carry conclusive answers pertaining to recognising and realising Love energy supporting all life? No, they do not. Nor were they ever trained to consider the questions being appropriately asked for promoting human benefit.

Their training is drawn from skittish knowledge. That means it has been relayed through routine methods of education, which rely on a recall of planetary detail in memory as a continuum for a resurrection or a reframing of past theorems. It has been acknowledged many times as a repetitive designing and aligning of a square wheel. Why would recall of the past inconsistencies be necessary? Academics are never capable of rounding the wheel of life into a circular shape of satisfactory measurement.

Planetary training in education today is limited by the universal rules of exploitative practices. These imposed methods of control deny an exploration of the mental states in psyche that lead to a cosmic connection with available access to the Greater Understanding of hidden Intelligence. The use of planetary belief systems have been deliberately designed to confuse and thus refuse the human mind and memory access to a more developed comprehension of their cosmic birthright and futurity heritage.

****

The Blue Print

If control is synonymous with self-mastery neither method has a future in the changing times leading to the reintroduction of planet Earth and its creatures into the cosmic sphere of the Fifth Dimension. What then of the presumed enlightenment of science overwhelming planetary minds? Has religious fervour and spiritual desires for ownership of much the same managed to clean or clear the slate for any of the countries where superstitious beliefs have manifested into different forms of worshipping icons?

It has been written that everybody dreams there is a better world somewhere waiting beyond this one in which people find their selves locked in harness from day to day. Dreams of this nature are not futuristic wishes; they are memories of a time when human energy was not incarcerated in this particular solar system.

The planet and its creatures were in what we call an incubation period in the Cosmos Proper. The Cosmos Proper is like an inner ring vibrating at certain tension levels or degrees, which cause a series of harmonics to reverberate through space to ease those who suffer from troubled minds.

Humans were designed and built in the Cosmos Proper and placed in a nursery to promote their initial growth. Planet Earth was built there also in that rhythmic space. Perhaps we could call it a world of future dreaming. Perhaps for some the visionary skills acquired could be seen as the birthing of imagination.

The initial human future was programmed by architects known cosmically as Ancients. The Ancients' role was to develop a particular portion of the Divine plan, where a set of blueprints went on their drawing board. We could say daily. What is the length of a day in cosmic terms? The Ancients can be seen as playing the role of cosmic architects. They were also into experimentation. However, such experiments were not always planned to the degree of measurement that suited everybody.

To give an analogy of present time journeying: the travellers are weary from the long journey and wish to arrive home to be greeted by family and friends. They are fed on arrival, given a place by the fire and a warm bed. This goes on for some time and the travellers begin to think this is a right and a privilege, which they evidently deserve. Then, one morning, they are handed an axe and shown a heap of wood, and told it is their turn to maintain the fire with enthusiasm.

Awakening to Living Energy

What would you do? Accept that life is about teamwork or spit the dummy and say that no one truly appreciates your hidden qualities of a prince or princess who will not deign to share in the practical workload of everyday.

****

Belonging

We remember those lost times when lovers were new
Where grasses grew greenest, skies were more blue
While walking paved pathways red roses we strew
And wild as the winds blew our sweet passion grew
When no words were spoken yet somehow we knew
Where Love gave us meaning hearts remained true

I know in some strange way we two still belong
Where rivers we played by still echo with song
Say not you love me for things may go wrong
Just keep holding my hand as we wander along
In crowds of lost people who muster and throng
Where richer is poorer and the weaker grow strong

While keys to life purpose do not give up a clue
The mindless seem locked in a room without view
Vain hopes they may search for are so far and few
Sad children wear clothing they have long outgrew
Though a secret belonging holds fast me and you
We cannot reach them while their heads are askew

Sweet voices advise these are loose times to spurn
Messages we bring through offer Love: they will learn
Our souls are linked elsewhere: so together we yearn
For the hearths of our Home where warm fires burn
There strong hearts and sure minds all oneness discern
Welcoming arms of The Divine Mother wait our return.

Chapter III

Profiling

The Unnamed One: *Our dedicated work is to break open the narrowed focus in mind and memory of human knowledge that is blinding present day consciousness. We are to bring the light of greater understanding into the world and create the connection of togetherness.*

Expanding the Bigger Picture

When each person can see more clearly what their life of programmed futurity depicts they will automatically break away from the malfunctioning moulded framework described as ego pretence. Ego influence has delivered reams of procrastinating self-esteem for the supposed benefit of recipients by well-meaning advice offered from whatever conniving, unchallenged sources dictated as terms of reality a long time ago.

There is a necessity for people today to find individual expression within, an evenly balanced stance on two feet, without the supporting crutches of an erroneously labelled ego persona. Thus removing the transfixed social habits of traditional values and so no longer remain as just another fixated herd animal lacking native instinct.

In other words, we must break apart the pitiable societal labels affixed to suit the whims of controlling miscreants. People raised in any culture subconsciously agree to wear labels of derangement and attachment to suit whatever pleases the whimsical attitudes of others seen as superior. Their occasional break away efforts for individuality are a futile attempt to provide support for a singular comfort zone, which only subjects them further towards the wasted material of prevailing social mores.

Cosmic Pioneers of Futurity Benefit

The aim of society pundits is for people to survive.
Our interest is focused on them becoming alive.

Unnamed One: This entity/energy symbolizing a singular portion of group energy that speaks with you reappeared on planet Earth in 1994. We have been here many times in planetary form over the past two and a half million years. We only come in significant times when shifts of major importance are necessitated for planet Earth and its subjectively estranged creatures nominated as human beings.

Everything noteworthy is connected in a certain sense. Therefore, we are time warped once more into promoting a futurity movement of planetary life from the third into the Fifth Dimension where we are obligated to offer a lead in Greater Understanding. The general flow of humanity will gradually follow in similar direction. That does not make us physical leaders of people in general. We can be seen as cosmic pioneers establishing futurity formats of Greater Understanding for communal benefits. At least that is how our supporting cosmic friends, the Angels, see us heading.

We can also be called the 37. We carry the energy of cosmic lighting and are conductors or conduits for energies in and beyond the cosmos who work through us in promoting human benefit.

We are not gods. Nor are we superior. Nor are we declared as prophets in a planetary sense. Though we carry visions of futuristic events, our work is mainly spent in spreading an understanding of greater energy. We understand the human systems that glorify and deify icons for their pecuniary methods of control and profiteering.

As the cosmic information we receive is forecasting energy sequences we are involved in writing essays and articles, poetry and some allegorical short stories. We have composed a small number of songs and ditties. We look forward to introducing ancient melodies that are presently situated in the backlog of human memory vaults called psyche.

Do you carry some vague genetic memory of having lived before? Well, because we are all eternal in spirit that would mean some form of energy shape shifting. At the level we work from that means an exchange of form. A different face. Another suit of clothes. Humans have a habit of reproducing each other in likeness. Does the eternal Living Energy, that which cannot die, reproduce the same effect in gathering wavelengths of perpetual strength? Of course it does.

Profiling

The spark or sparkle of beyond planetary life energy is obvious in the lighted eyes of all living creatures. The spirit within being is observable to those who are interested enough to look without seeking advantage. It is a light of awareness that dances without restraint. Observe the dulled eyes of one whose breath of life has gone elsewhere. Where is the spark of energy? What is not apparent to those who deny humans of their cosmic essence is that the light carries the beam of inner consciousness; thus demonstrating life giving streams of Cosmic Intelligence.

Excessive amounts of decaying book knowledge have deadened the inquiring minds of little people. Sophistication has fattened and made lazy the mental muscles designed for an expansive inquiry into futurity. We laugh with some humour because we have come to trim the impurities from between the over-educated ears of those classified as socially superior.

We are, amongst many other various attributes, trainers in promoting the mental skills of advanced Intelligence. We are here to assist humans to stand firmly on their feet, free of wobbling mental restrictions called doubtful mien. The rational mind is burdened down with fabrications, which in the area of psychotherapy we call ego manipulation. It is like an outer skin covering, which should have been shed or washed clear away a long time ago.

Why does it remain as a ploy of mental hindrance? Because society leaders bought a protection plan, a long time ago on time payment in iconic thinking called religiosity. Clearly, this has never been able to reduce the overburden of related liabilities. In the next few years, all universal indebtedness will be forgiven. How much weight will that remove from the worried minds and shoulders of a work weary populace struggling to gain an understanding of human worth.

We have a magnificent series of stories to tell of the birthing and continuation of developing the human species in their journey back to Home. The following tale of the descent of Lucifer and his comrades called the 37 who put the early human species initially on their two planetary feet is only one among many.

Where amongst the maddened throng of society dwellers is the missing one known as The Unnamed prodigal son? Why did Christianity and other type cast religions not derive a conclusion to make four? The best they could ever manage was three, which leaves the bigger picture demonstrating life incomplete. What if the visitation of Jesus 2000 years ago left subtle messages within the scattered stones of a destroyed Jerusalem society? Messages that were ignored, suggesting there was a greater source underlying his visitation Have synagogues and other religious institutions ever tried to make headway in interpreting them?

We that speak with you are not encased in human form though some of us at various times temporarily wear the covering of human skin. We offer you and fellow readers a rare opportunity to communicate with cosmic learning, which is a Greater Understanding of life and living free ranging far beyond the limited scope of planetary knowledge.

Are you a seeker of the eternal flame of blue energy we nominate as Light of Intelligence? Alternatively, are you a mere reflection of the conservative rehashed versions that most of the global articles demonstrating the confines of dubious knowledge partially portray as factual? We offer to you an opportunity to share in carrying a flame of brilliant light that outshines the symbolism the Olympic torch is universally signifying.

****

Cosmic Interlocutors

We are nominated as cosmic interlocutors. We are deliberately trained by Angels and those of Greater Energy whose intention delivers messages of Love and Intelligence to benefit the varied races of people existing on planet Earth. We are required to advise those prepared to listen that their harried times of third dimensional pain and pressure is very close to ending.

On behalf of the Great Mother energy, we offer a smooth rearrangement of being to realize a shift into the Fifth Dimension. We are suitably trained to mentally assist those willing to join the oncoming movement into the outer realms of the Cosmos Proper.

We, this small coterie of cosmic pioneers installed on planet Earth, have assisted in breaking through the veil of mystery that has hidden the meaning of life embracing Love energy for eons. As such we are bonded in Love with the Divine and Great Mother. We have been given the keys to delivering the importance of engaging three vital principles into a living arrangement.

Therefore, we are set the task of delivering cosmic understandings and sharing the tremendous wealth stored for future human benefit in Truth, Unity, and Equality. By entering into such meaningful discussions, participating people will come to terms with an understanding of who they are and their future purpose in further defining and refining cosmic creativity.

It is necessary to understand the difference between activation and involvement. We are subject to the workings of the Divine Plan. As such, we do not manipulate. As activists, we have an interest in generating newfound energy through developing measures in Greater Understanding for the express purpose of promoting human welfare. Involving ourselves in human affairs of the state, such as diverse political opinion, will lessen the strength we are building to further the intentions of the Divine Plan.

****

Channelling

Channelling is a mental form of interactive communication beyond the crudity of third dimensional thought processing. All people receive channelled information through mind in varying degrees or measures. Most are not aware that thought can be drawn from so many different areas that are not immediately apparent in rational memory. Many deny they receive messages that are not being drawn from their surface memory banks for fear of an insanity labelling. When channelling occurs, it is similar to a transmission of radio short waves that are being received by a setting tuned to that particular frequency. Basically, there are two major forms of channelling. First and mostly, messages are received silently in mind and then relayed by the person who is open to the dimensional contacts, secondly where they actually speak through the persona and the recipients are thus seen as mediums.

Luxor and Jézel are intergalactic channels, both bearing cosmic initiated names, both designed as human entities in this Common Era, and their arrival on the Earthly stage began this time on the planet some 30 years ago. They also embody the Unnamed Energy and so carry the endorsement of the Greater Unnamed energy. Cosmic entity/energies use mind telepathy. When they work and speak with and through Jézel and Luxor, they often use persona imagery so it is accepted as an area of balance. Talking through and relating understandings conveyed by cosmic entity/energies require teamwork.

Luxor is not a prophetic entity in the normal usage of the word. Sometimes he is prescient and subject to visions. Most of the time, the advanced information he receives and employs is mentally channelled from renowned cosmic sources such as Angels. We refer to the energy sources as people who carry no specific names. In the interest of discerning the different areas of communications, and bounded by the limitations of third dimensional language, we are required to use planetary labels for identification purposes. This method is performed within Luxor in a series of sensory inputs until a recognizable pattern is formatted. It is another form of cosmic channelling.

Jézel, for 25 years, has been the preferred medium for verbal presentations from cosmic levels, the agreement of which was made some eons ago. The vibration for transmission comes through the crown chakra and the messages are relayed through using the frontal lobes of the mind/brain as a transmitter, something like a CB radio frequency. The messengers appear through her in the form of a character. She is aware of what is being said and has some later recall. As they begin to converse the mind of Jézel moves inwardly so she can offer planetary information mentally to them while the relayed session is in progress. She is not able to participate in the discussion verbally, because they are using her vocal chords aligned with her body system to express the imparted messages. Jézel does not have a say as to when they will come through, though there are agreed times when we wish certain cosmic energies to be present.

Jézel has channelled in the main many cosmic entity/energies. The discussions are held in the English language, at which they are adept, though we are aware that they also have the use of other languages, which they sometimes use in between chatting sessions. Some exchanges occur from beyond cosmic such as Beyond the Beyond and the Shining Ones who were instrumental in designing and developing the star systems occupying the galaxies.

The purposes of discussion carry manifolds. There is a constant projection of Love energy radiating through and around this planet Earth. It is to create Greater Understandings for the participating players on the planet, of which there are many. The arena is also used as a training platform for many Angels who have never been involved on planet Earth before. It is an opportunity for them to extend their levels of understanding. The Angels convey to us the message that we are never alone. While the discussions are in full swing, there is always a cosmic group of interested students observing various forms of human culture.

The conversations by agreement have been digitally recorded and in earlier times were also videoed. The processing has been in operation for more than twenty-five years. There are probably more than 2,000 hours of recorded conversations, though at present, Luxor and Jézel are mostly fed cosmic information where necessary for upgrades, such as the unfolding of the New Day and the Fifth Dimensional level becoming more apparent.

The information received covers wide ranging topics that contain much of what would be considered spiritual revelations on this planet were we of religious intent, which we are not.

It is important to understand that we are not religiously bent, that we do not indulge in worshipping icons, though we are interested in rearranging some of the stories told in the Bible, a variety of misconstrued scriptures, where they relate to previous activities that reference those who we represent. Why have we waited for twenty odd years preferring not to broadcast this information globally even though it is not considered secretive material?

We talk to people who are prepared to listen and allow the exchanges to alter and rearrange their patterned lives. However, there are very few at this stage who have moved beyond the levels of superstitious fears to allow themselves the competency to clearly hear what is being stated cosmically.

That which we speak extensively on is the development of The New Mind for advancing human endeavour and the movement of dimensions affecting the planet and therefore human futurity. This we nominate as the dawning of The New Day into the Fifth Dimension.

****

A New Understanding

Lucifer speaks:

We reiterate that we are the children of the Great Mother energy. We endorse and will further enforce the work areas we are required to deliver. It has been stated we are cosmic pioneers. It is our job to move ahead to establish work points of Greater Understanding so that humans can follow the cosmic lead.

We do not take on board the stale ego pretence that humans are prone to encapsulate. It is not for us to use the hackneyed phrase 'I am'. It is not even for us to say who we are. It is enough for us to realize who we are and implement our work commitment. We do not have a requirement to broadcast that knowing to people in general. As advised by Greater Energy, the cosmic material we have been trained to interpret and relate is destined to be broadcast globally.

Who, except the Great Mother, knows that which she wishes to have conveyed as Divine Womanhood? Yes, we have had inklings. We do not yet know how to portray Womanhood from its area of foundation. Training areas will be provided later for those who will promote aspects of Divine Womanhood, because what has been demonstrated on the planet to date as female frames of ownership fall far short of that which demonstrates the Great Mother's declared level of Divine Womanhood.

Awakening to Living Energy

Then what of revealing Intelligence? That which The One shared for the benefit of cosmic understanding as the three principles of Truth, Unity, and Equality. Those three principles were declared and written in the stars a very long time ago and remain eternally present. So who be it planetary or be it cosmically ordained, has stepped up to understand and embrace the meaning, the fulfilment of those three principles? The simple answer at this stage is no one carries the understanding.

The Great Mother clearly understands Intelligence. Those who have come from the Great Ocean have the understanding within, but not those who have come after The One nor those who stand behind waiting for others to lead. They do not as yet have the comprehension of what is meant for futurity by observing the three principles.

At this stage, we, those of us presently on the planet, are caught in a cleft stick, if you like, which means that our minds are split between what we have learned from inherited areas of knowledge and that which we have come to realize cosmically. We, as conduits, do not pretend to have full understanding of where we have come from and where we are being guided, and whether we personally will find some form of completion in this specific journey undertaken.

So it is frustrating to those with unclear minds and memory, is it not? For on one hand we know or realize far more than any average human mind can comprehend, or, if you like, we are given to understand so much more of the cosmic worlds. Yet on the other hand, we do not as yet have an opportunity to meet the conditions of a new world. What we know with certainty is that, anyone who is enclosed within this planetary or cosmic bubble, has yet to experience being released from what might be termed conditioning.

Therefore, those who wag their tongues from their overloaded minds about being able to touch base with unconditional love are cheats, liars, flagrant poseurs, and wasted storytellers, who pretend to be what they can never hope to achieve. Love does not wear different versions to suit people's flagrant ideas of superiority.

There can be no such objective as Love is, nor that Love is not. Love energy is not subject to duality phrasing. Love encompasses all. It is not subject to planetary forms of conditioned responses. As for promoting Intelligence, its roots of foundation are set firmly in Love energy.

Many people on the planet are classified as intellectual, but it is a trained system of recalling cycled knowledge. It does not have access to the basic understanding of knowing, which is worth. When you wish to become one who is an aligned knower of Intelligence then you will wipe your mental slate clean of the lingering memory frames of disputed knowledge.

Modern memories have been described as a dusty surface covering that coats the mirror of past indulgences. We will tell you clearly that for those who are religious, those who are of scientific bent, those who are caught up in the everyday whims of societal fashion, the self-reflective mirror is an important part of revealing true status within. We advise you to clearly smash the surface mirrors of ill repute.

Those of us who are charged with bringing through the new understandings of light energy as humans move progressively into the Fifth Dimension, have no need to carry disfigured mirrors of self-indulgence. We will access futurity measures by smashing the lingering stained mirrors of past indulgences. As those who support us cosmically have already smashed theirs into oblivion. For those who have not, they are still caught in whirlpools that cycle and recycle their lingering areas of pressure and pain.

The future for all is to get on board with the spiralling effect that lifts us from the known into the unknown and draws us inexorably towards realizing the greater unknowable energy residing within being.

Uncompleted Rhapsody

Something in your eyes
Looks like you and me
Oh, what sweet surprise
When we can finally see
That our hearts and mind
Determined from above
Were always of the kind
To be enjoined in love

Something in your eyes
Oh, tell me it is true
Things that I surmise
Are recognised in you
The sparkle that I saw
Was a momentary ignite
Of a mighty fiery roar
Setting worlds alight

Something in your face
Brings every star to bind
Makes our minds erase
Tears we leave behind
Never will be some time
Beyond yon sweet recall
When the dream sublime
Gathers in the all.

Written by Luxor on the morning of Jézel's birthday - 07/02/09

Awakening to Living Energy

Chapter IV

The Product is You

The Unnamed One: *It is an uncanny instinct in human frailty that people will continually close their minds and rail or protest against receiving fresh information on understanding what it is they say they desire most from life; for example love, peace, friendship, democracy, freedom, justice, etc.*

Cosmic Food on Offer

In our daily working practice we eat of the same food from the same cosmic table as that which we are instructed to offer to be shared with others as a mutual benefit.

This food of Greater Understanding we offer carries a beneficence to improve human welfare that is without parallel in opportunities. It presents a series of cosmic designed programs to progress the stature of human thoughts and action into more expansive panoramas of future visionary talent. It carries that which we classify as open realms of Greater Understanding, Life purpose and Living Free arrangement.

The first step to achieving such highly prized situations is to confer with an awareness of who you are representing, being different from what you are considered to be in society values. To do this exercise of revelation one must learn the artistry of mentally diving deeper into the unconscious world of the psyche, which holds fast the pearls beyond price underlying the futurity purpose in planetary being.

Using that quality style of mental submergence the enquiring mind moves into flashes of cosmic memory. This is where there is a remembrance of deliberate lines of cosmic purpose, which initially brought the ancestry in human form onto this planet. Such relative information is readily available in memory for those who are trained to know where to research.

Awakening to Living Energy

We remind people that we do not carry particular answers for them specifically. Answers are your hidden gifts waiting for you to internally discover, uncover and recover. That is not to say we are not capable of glimpsing where you are collectively situated in the given moment or observe futurity areas where we are heading.

There are questions within being waiting to be explored and examined and responses without conditioning made available for future mental digestion. Ready-made answers are the glib retorts of knowledgeable experts in whatever industry they represent. Scientists are adept at giving far-reaching answers without any recognisable substance of intelligent design.

We are competently trained to set people on a suitable course of personal rearrangement as well as advising in such matters as where to look for future signposts signalling the variety of bends in the homeward journey. And yes, we do offer a backup plan if you are in need of an occasional push, but it is not our job to lead you unnecessarily on your journey of achieving greater understanding, or for that matter to hold your hand when occasionally the going ahead gets rugged or rough.

In the gathering of Intelligence pertinent to human futurity growth you are required to break open the fallow ground lodged within your innate self, assisted by whatever specific cosmic information we are advised to convey to you. The alternative to that which is being offered, is that you will remain attached to the singularity of the clustered human herd mentality without the specialised strength available to build the necessary growth in personal delivery through entering the next stage of individual character.

The outcome following the progression of individual character ultimately leads to advanced standards of supramental thought processing, which we nominate as a tertiary achievement of building worth into wholeness of being. We are beyond cosmically trained in recognising and removing the cobwebs cluttering the DNA memory banks, which currently hold the advancement of Intelligence of planetary people in abeyance. We can provide extra energy until students can acknowledge and clear what it is that still chokes their localised memory. These incidental features can be seen as delaying hindrances, detrimental to achieving futurity growth patterns.

The cobwebs or weeds in memory, as we call them, are remnants from past life encounters, haphazard adventures, plus unresolved issues in fragmented family lines. These issues were never brought to fruition in previous lifetimes and so continue to dog the unresolved strands of hereditary DNA strains.

These loose ends, inaccurately deemed by superior minds as weakness in character building are to be brought to the surface, mentally refurbished into new strengths of character, and then joined in a mutual bonding with what is already established as being free and clear of prevailing belief patterns in society.

The opportunity is open for each to seize the unforgiving moment and move successfully onto an amazing mental free way of Greater Understanding. There is the opportunity to achieve an inner acuity that moves all thought processing beyond normal human comprehension.

It is a necessary step we each must take towards fulfilling our portion of a vital destiny awaiting the projected awakening of the human races. It is the same road of Greater Understanding that those demonstrating genius levels of performance have taken previously. Inevitably, it is an open invitation to access a free way of undertaking that eventually leads us back to Home.

In the meanwhile, there is much exciting work for each voluntary pioneer to perform. There are many global fields of industry where we are required to develop influential treatment to rebuild hate-filled societies into friendly communities willing to nurture humane consideration for all people regardless of race or credo.

The Time of Cosmic Awakening

We are intent on gathering together investitured companions, those of the half million transplanted pioneers who are not too tired or exhausted to express willingness, so we may further establish and maintain the stages of progressive facilitation already set in motion through the deliverance of New Day activities.

There is the light of a very bright star is waiting for each of us to follow through in our undertaking of responsible growth. This will guide us in completing our mutual courses and causes in the nominated period of awakening over the next few years. With the realization arriving of Beings-in-Love, which rearrangements should those awakened early be making to view a new chapter in life and interact with present group surroundings?

Wholeness through Willingness

The willingness to allow fault lines in the subconscious levels to surface and be cleansed of dross clears away the uncertainties affecting the rational mind that leads to unwanted and unwarranted incidents. Through this determination of spirit, the portent of accidents and illness can be nullified or removed from the human system.

Awakening to A New Mind and Living Free begins when joy and understanding replaces the outmoded systems of opposing forces of duality at work in ego practice. The two selves, the actor on the planetary stage and the cosmic lead player within soul energy are to merge into becoming one individual in character.

The door to the internal energy of fire is opened and available to access by those who show the willingness to understand what is meant by the absorption of Love Energy. It is through cosmic arrangement and agreement that the next level of human intelligence, the factoring of A New Mind, and the rewiring of depleted brain cells will open to operate at speeds that surpass the everyday formats of educational plodding.

Summary

Beyond every faltering persona, there is a greater program of Intelligence sealed in the memory banks of psyche willed and waiting the opportunity to emerge and converge in linked agreement with the two selves denoting presence and essence.

Such a unified program will only appear effectively when the partitioning wall maintaining the dual separation of two selves is dismantled and agreement to become as one is implemented through a connective mind procedure.

Part of our programmed work sessions is demonstrating how easy and simple a reintroduction of twin entities back into a role of individual wholeness can be achieved simply through the application of willingness in mind and memory. No longer will people be compelled by maladjustment to live as two strangers in the same mental house indifferent in attitude to the conflicting variances inflicting fear and pain on other portions of the human system.

The history of human existence began two and a half million years ago when measured in linear time. What is the purpose behind the journey that runs from here to there and then on from where to nowhere in particular to eventually realize our inevitable destiny is the return to a cosmic home from whence our journey of self-discovery first began?

****

The Emerging Product is Within You

There are widened gaps between planetary systems and cosmic levels of advancement. We intend to fill that voided space with dedicated themes of mental growth we call the Product. The Product is of vital concern to validate you because the rearrangement of diverse systems in question is bearing cosmic fruit that is ripening within each of us.

It is a complex situation in mind and memory. The goodies being offered for future show time are already embedded within our internal systems. We are to mentally dive into the hidden depths in psyche to gain access to futurity benefits. What are these fore-mentioned goodies?

Goodies are the futurity release of programmed systems located in the hidden wells of psyche, which require identification and an acknowledgement of willingness for a granted elevation to attain understanding on the surface level in mind and memory.

Everything we might wish to grant us wholeness in spirit energy is enclosed within our innermost being. Humans have looked longingly outside of self to fulfil their dreaming state of wishful thinking. We call this skimming on thin ice in the present-day surface programming. There are deeper programs lodged within the psyche demanding the opportunity of wakening for futurity expression. Our job as cosmic pioneers is to dive inwardly and enable access to the hidden areas, thus making them visually understandable and available for personal growth, and eventually, public survey.

When we want our personal planting of futurity programming to flourish, we need to first check out our basic rooted (past) systems. They are situated at subterranean levels, well below the turbulent waters of normal society consciousness. The wedges and ledges that stop people promoting fresh activity in mind and brain development involve removing sordid beliefs harbouring wilful dreams of choice, freedom, freewill and unconditional love sorties.

Fourth dimensional levels are full of misconceptions, illusion and disillusionment, or in today's parlance, misinformation, fake news, and persistent conspiracy theories.

We are to continue to dig, dive and die to everyday conditioning for each entity form to embrace personal programs of futurity development. Dying inwardly is a doorway or portal to enter new levels of advanced consciousness beyond the triteness locked down in theoretical scenarios of everyday misconceptions called scientific knowledge.

Innate Intelligence

It is interesting to understand that the innate self is just as competent as the proportional ego self to argue for its particular area of advancement.

Awakening to Living Energy

What that means is that the ego self is universally built because if it were to be coming from the cosmic beyond as we understand it, there would be no argument involved in duality. Therefore, disagreements are dimensional areas or levels, and in the returning journey to Home, which is Love ordained, we each have to traverse those non-compliant gradients beguiling the progression of soul energy.

The planetary framework of insecure living styles societies are burdened with today carries a massive load of quantitative knowledge that first broaches and then belittles or scorns the innate structuring promoting human intelligence.

Beliefs are mental blockages that refuse to allow access to Intelligence, which is innate energy within each self. To move into the unconscious zone of memory requires certain degrees of harmless innocence to access the void of nothingness. You cannot just move from the ego system or status level of pretence by saying, 'I will access the depth of unconscious cognition'. It just does not happen like that.

You are to dive within your subconscious until you find a mind level that is impervious to selfish dreams of planetary advantage. In which case you will realize the influence of daily mind controls and conditioning nominated as ego is left behind.

Ego has no area available for realising Greater Understandings that build from a cosmic foundation. What ego does master are frames of mental control; typified by rude displays of impatient pettiness built on platforms of ignorance and arrogance, which carry as much potent energy as dream castles floating in the sky. When you are capable of coming to that realization then you will no longer give supplication to the ever-demanding religious god sense featuring misguided ethics, morals and virtues.

The innate intelligence we offer to share is greater, more expressive, more fulfilling in content than any strictured ego platitudes can dream up. The wide spread of energy in understanding we speak of is vastly beyond the narrow perceptions of life and living standards that any ego status is prepared to offer.

Humans have a depth of history that the ego-controlled mind cannot fathom and so therefore refuses to justify research into areas beyond the shallow cognisance of knowledge being expressed in everyday schooling. The ego wants to amplify its right to control the surface mind by superimposing the conditional stamp of whatever is overriding who you are at this present age.

To maintain its stance, it continually projects side tracking ideas into the mind of whatever you are intent on transacting. The narrow or focused minded ones are then in return expected to bow and endorse what is being dished up onto their plates as suspect facts of life, statements of dubious value that are not open to questioning.

When you build the strength of individual character within self, you can say to ego framing, 'Buddy, what you have been feeding me to date is akin to bullshit. I come from a line of energy greater than anything you have to offer.' Arguments will subside when the ego pretence stops frothing and blustering in its bullying manner to control situations. Then it most probably will say, 'Okay, I wondered when you would get around to understanding due procedures. As such I acknowledge I am a manager assisting you in passing through this period of life you are involved in progressing.' Having established the supporting role it was always meant to play the ego can become a worthwhile companion instead of it proclaiming a role of pretentious tyranny.

The ego then becomes a manager willing to ensure you operate appropriately in advancing the conscious mental system. Until you have the guts to confront the ego and tell it you are mature enough take the reins in further developing mind and memory, and that you require its endorsement through recognising your greater field of energy, the ego will continue to kick the shit out of your planning whenever it so pleases.

The Angels and Ancients have called the present involved situations for humans a roller coaster ride. We see it like a ride on a bucking horse where you continue to hang on while being internally bruised because you are too afraid to let go and jump off. There is any number of suitable analogies that express the fear of engaging in that which is unknown.

When you receive the reins of stability in mind, be sure to hand them across to The Divine Mother so that the Angels will attend to your next rite of passage.

****

Explosion of Soul Energy

The birthing of fresh energy within mind and memory begins with endorsing the concept of a three into one package we promote as a product for futurity development.

The modern mind of civilized power is loosely scattered because it does not carry a benchmark for locating foundation in being. The new foundation for Life and Living free begins with a broader understanding of the essential you that is calling into question an understanding of the mysterious 'who'. To achieve a sense of inner balance we are required to merge the heart of soul essence with the innate presence in a new mind development.

The merging of essence and presence delivers the unified strength of oneness. The energy within is an explosion of soul energy in line with the Awakening to A New Mind (being in mental agreement) that is being matched by soul energy becoming more apparent as people move progressively into the Fifth Dimension.

The ego pretence is required to relinquish control of the occupied mental system. Today the ego related presence and soul essence are in states of separation. The ego pretence became isolated in active role-playing and goal setting and separated from soul energy. The ego system is thus seen as a breakaway movement from wholeness.

It was initially built to give children a helping hand, to stand ready and steady, and secure in finding their own feet. Ego was meant to be a servant and was very good at what it initially conveyed, but in the splitting or separation of mind from the core energy of soul ego became masterful, controlling and perversely corruptible. *The Parable of Jésu - the story of servants and masters.*

The destiny for human energy is Home. Many childhood games were played about reaching a home base as an end result and the motivating force in playing such games is to reach a satisfactory conclusion. A memory of Home is located within the depths of every being.

****

Stand in Light

In these present day times
Religions lose their energy
God sense has been relegated
A return to natural order
Not where vain man ordains

Now each person is required
To stand in a portion of light
No longer is the shadow of god
Meant to cast an artificial glow

Atheists were formed by denial
Not recognising any god within
Their focus is directed outward
Invariably they are pyramid seekers

When balance replaces duality
The jaundiced eye of ego sense
Is cleansed and then nullified
Allowing the diamond to surface

In the equality of balance
We are lifted and lightened
In the resolvement of pairing
There is awareness that strife
Has formed from cosmic life
What has been called mystery
Is a loss of address to memory

While entities ride the night skies
Ancient energy is buried within
Without any given comprehension
Advising the rational waking state

Those who have glorified
The rationality of mind
Can now rest, reassured
When we lose that state
There is no longer loss
The image people perceive
Mirrors the lack of birthright

Tradition is for glorification
A perpetuation of past mistakes
Only the righteous and moral
Cannot perceive the errors
Within their own judgement
Condemning others to repeat them

Religions maintain a dance of cycle
Where lovers of ritual are prisoners
Needing no external warders
Willingly they turn their own keys
Kissing the pale hand of their jailer, death

Authority sans wisdom is a cold master
Controlling influences are governors
Restricting the innate abilities within
To spread their wings of expression
Mere speculations are messy affairs
Idol assumptions masking the obvious

Mystery stirs the soul in depths
Where desire cries out for unity
Within is mirrored a futured past
That we are is enough to know

More than that is icing on a cake
Prepared with truth and equality
Seeking wisdom to be performed
By sitting still with an empty plate

Grace is the dew of warm oblivion
Releasing one from time and space
Without the controlling ego mind
Love and beauty take their place

Awakening to Living Energy

Chapter V

Promoting Personal Futurity

The Unnamed One: *Each moment in time holds memory and each movement we deliberately make foretells a future happening.*

The Birthing

Endorsing the birthing of new energy levels sealed within the human system of psyche begins through embracing the three in one growth program outlining Promoting Personal Futurity.

These essays we offer for consideration are not some flash in the pan overnight gizmos set to tantalise tired mental taste buds; only to be dropped off later on to be replaced with an avaricious glimpsing that suggests something else is even bigger, better and brighter on radar to enhance the blinkered eyes involved in exploiting everyday affairs.

The advanced information provided derives from carefully compiled and tested theories of mental programming, over-viewed, worked through thoroughly, and tested successfully over the past twenty-five years. This data has been inducted by some of the most qualified minds whose expertise in Greater Understanding have uncovered latent areas of importance missing in both philosophy and psychology determinations. The material we offer is pertinent to further developing human intellect into advanced measures of quantum intelligence exceeding the limitations of present day recorded knowledge.

The conclusions drawn from such extensive researching state that when certain principles relevant to Life and Living Free are mentally introduced and activated, constructed accurately, and accepted willingly, then a certain amount of brain waves presently residing dormant in the mental human system awakens. They further transform or rearrange present day thinking patterns into fresh bursts of colourful cosmic awareness in being,

The relevant information once made available opens avenues into latent memories that have been shut down for eons by the overuse and abuse of inducted erroneous piecemeal configurations. These have been deemed to be the last word in scientific research formally demonstrating as planetary knowledge.

Simply put, the advance payments in future mind development promoting human intellect is still locked in the psyche banks we call hidden vaults of advanced cosmic memory. When the futuristic programs for human development were initially lodged, the doors to the memory vaults were slammed shut and the combination of numbers for release spun haphazardly. The correct sequential timing set in opening the mental apparatus is not practically available until there is a combined readiness in acceptance, a willingness in activated human minds to apply for greater individual benefits detailing advanced methods of Greater Understanding.

So for those who are willing to engage their innate systems in new social levels of improved mental health, in the enrichment of wealth in Greater Understanding, as well as an enduring relationship appreciation they can attain on average a 100% increase in mental acuity skills in a very short while. The ball of future communal benefits advancing mind skills of cosmic awareness is already bouncing in the human forecourt just waiting to be hit!

The exponential increases on offer work from what is a starting point, a cosmic benchmark that is already established beyond the knowledgeable framework of local memory operative within lackaday personas. Developing a greater clarity in advanced thought processing at this stage is styled as individual in effort and is not meant to make everyone equal.

Rather it can be seen as working in a chain reaction style to make some singular or herd mentality enclosed people realize there are opportunities to step up and access an individual level of status. Thus moving advanced students of learning procedures into becoming team players working with defined strategies to promote communal living standards into a grander beneficial scale of Greater Understanding.

Beyond that degree then, there are levels of genuine equivalence available for more serious players, determined in their efforts to locate and open up unrealized areas of productivity referencing cosmic waves of Intelligence growth. Such effort in turn produces new formats of mental life skills, compatible energy available to further develop elements of even Greater Understanding advancing the delayed efforts providing communal benefit.

****

The Purpose of Future Human Growth

When the overviewing Angel approval was granted, the allocation of A New Mind sequence was cosmically lit and aligned for human benefit.

For the purpose of advancing futurity growth in cosmic development, there is a requirement to connect and merge the planetary mind and brain with the internal cosmic energy resource nominated as soul essence. There is a necessity to develop a broader understanding of how Love energy works to readjust misalignments of consciousness and thus complement a balancing process within the human system. The foundation of Love energy is the Home base for releasing and rearranging emotional and mental instability that has been framed into conditional human thinking by any number of inaccurate belief patterns.

To supersede the state of mental duality that is rapidly reaching its use by date, there is a requirement for an understanding of that which is cosmically meant as worth. The ambiguous questions located in duality-type thinking locks the minds of people into diverse states of singularity. No way does the ego's influence on persona agreeably allow the rational mind access into studying purpose in individuality, which when acknowledged, offers a tertiary course of Greater Understanding to develop advanced grades of cosmic intelligence.

People are to move beyond the twin states of duality nominated as opposites within the conditioned mind of ego management. They are to marry and merge these varied differences to achieve a modicum of balance thus promoting degrees of competency. Defining and merging differences in the human framework, one called ego/esteem and the other internal self/worth is necessary to allow the processing of the everyday mind to compete and complete a satisfactory transfer to the newly awakening cosmic related mind.

The production of the new cosmic mind supersedes our present day logically based rational mind. There is an automatic follow through development determining the progression of recovery allowing an internal discovery and uncovering of lost records pertaining to developing communal human welfare.

A companion anthology speaks of these developed forms of Greater Understanding in simplified forms through stories, symbols, and a collection of rhyming verse.

Awakening to Living Energy

As they stand immersed and stupefied in recurring beliefs of the specified ego driven god sense in religious fervour, immature people can only present like small children on an isolated shore, gazing at a cosmic ocean teeming with living features and creatures that stretch far beyond their limited range of imagination. People as programmed creatures for cosmic inclusion are amphibious. They are meant to plunge headlong into depthing the deep blue sea of psyche memory. Who is prepared to dive there to greet their future cosmic designation?

We do not wish to impress ideas on gullible people; rather we work to remove dubious impressions out of immature minds. Impressions are indentations that impair the natural progression of individual worth into wholeness of being. When minds become open to a memory recall of past events from other lives or times, they can often develop vague or obscure patterns from memory that are outwardly viewed as melancholy or depressive.

Too many psychotherapists through using modern medical opinions have sold a biased story that a depressed state of mind as they call it is harmful because it seems to ignore or reject patterns of socially approved connectivity. We view these temporary situations as a pause of internal reflection that is beneficial if it can run its short course in memory recall without interference from others using labels of guilt or remorse for traumatic effect.

****

Many Sizes in Personal Development

Living in joyous mode, devoid of fears fashioned from an accumulation of mental disorder, is simply accomplished within an undivided self.

We recommend shifting from external training methods into accessing internal depthing of mind and memory.

Promoting personal development for futurity benefit means what it says: The elemental mind is required to expand in conscious awareness from the beleaguered persona styled ego system. Paradoxically, it has to come to terms with the maxim that smaller in size equates with bigger surrounds. The external training methods that follow the building of knowledge and social habits form on the ego presence as a crusty, skin-deep layer.

Where the emphasis is allowed to remain with exploiting exterior glamour then bias develops subconscious areas of pressured pain and fear arising from deep-seated memories of past areas of destruction. If these areas are not suitably

Promoting Personal Futurity

addressed and cleared from mind and memory then accidents and illness will certainly manifest. Life is then experienced in staggered states of mental wobbling called duality that does not allow time out for suitable restful phases and peace in the stillness of mind.

The depth of inner resources of Life is meant to be plumbed. There are hidden profundities within each of us that no amount of external goodwill measures in habitual training methods can possibly locate. In poetic analogy, these areas are guarded and protected by fire-breathing dragons that will not release the pearls beyond price to those who are determined to stubbornly remain uninitiated. The pearls are meant for each to obtain on request yet these dragons of the mind cannot be wilfully slain by the greediness demonstrating planetary desires for ownership.

They are a part of memory cells or wells that reside in the hidden depths of psyche. When science and religions deny the socially bred humans their childhood fantasies they lock up the memory of dragon energy. No amount of practical denial can erase their deep-seated images. No amount of rationalization will bring into being the shimmering light of the New Day dawning. Each of us must locate the dragons of subliminal fear and balance in mind with the acknowledgement of greater energy to gather in the withheld pearls of wisdom offering future communal benefits.

Humans are in the early process of being given an opportunity to develop an expanded mind to override the existing ego system and duality regression that has outworn its usefulness. To receive the benefit of Greater Understanding, there is a requirement to do a personal mind inventory and discharge of beliefs that each of us was trained to on carry as hardened mindsets. If beliefs are seen as valid in mindfulness then they can be converted into advanced forms of knowing and are then useful allies in the forthcoming futurity growth. If they are not suitable then they should be summarily tossed. How does one ascertain life differences if a mental fear of the unknown sward refuses access to the necessary files maintained in the psyche? There is the dilemma besetting the gatekeeper role of ego occupying the vagaries of rational minds.

The New Mind entering into the Fifth Dimension is to be clear of the contamination of fear and pain resident in memory cells. As Jésu stated 2000 years ago, 'No one puts new wine into old wine skins lest they burst. They do not put old wine into new wine skins lest they spoil.' What are the belief patterns of the western world today when it comes to the sagacity accorded to Jésu? That he was the son of god and thus supported the religious folly of Yahweh worshippers? Not so. That he was no more than an ordinary man displaying a range of good intentions? Again it is not so. That he did not even exist? Denial does not make the recurring dreams of yesteryear happenings tend to go away.

The information available for achieving advanced personal benefits leads the rational mind of persona into exploring new levels of intelligent understanding transcending the backlog of practical knowledge called education. Thus mentally motivated energy fields within the human system are opened to promote the necessary means for improved mental health, enrichment of wealth in Greater Understanding, plus an enduring relationship of endearing quality.

When people are able to see clearly their own lodged difficulties, they will mentally collate the essential material to disperse what is listed as wasteful detritus. They will no longer rely on the advisory words of presumptuous type experts; nor have a need to listen to foolish words of advice from others intent on leading their lives further astray from achieving measures of Greater Understanding.

Personal development is about releasing the shadows that follow the memory in mind and dog everyday bewitching thoughts, which in turn, impede the growth of individual status. The simplified work required to greet A New Day and Living Free can be shown to each of you. The initial hard yards of retraining memory banks into denoting futurity measures are to be done individually; as one size does not fit all. And 'will thee or nil thee', at some stage the promotion of A New Mind into being assuredly will be seen to be done. When are you prepared to throw away the wasted baggage of old mind patterning and start living a new and exciting Fifth Dimensional existence?

****

Letting Go of Humanism

Some comments on the complexities of human conduct

The New Mind, when awakening within being, tends to conflict with the projected self-sabotaging efforts of ego esteem.

People that form their idiotic ideas of what are presumed successful performances from platforms of self-belief are little more advanced in theory than cretins. Mix in their polite company by all means, but do not enjoin with their pluralistic methods of herd type thinking. In other words, stay clear of the glue of attachment they convey when vocally they indulge in the braying spread of bullshit proclaiming self-belief is somehow the creditable answer in attaining successful living styles.

Learn to use minor setbacks as they unfold as an opportunity to dive deeper into the subconscious levels of memory and recover that described as hidden pearls. We suggest these can be symbolized as wisdom and beauty. Remember that inner knowing supersedes the vacuous airing of self-indulged knowledge.

What most people think that they know for certain, they keep smugly hidden from public scrutiny. Whatever it is they do not know conclusively, they tend to be over-fond of sharing such beliefs with others to hopefully gain a more advantageous clarity.

Those who voluntarily undertake work to accept the cosmic mind of Greater Understanding will be streets ahead of those who compulsorily have to wear the planetary overload of daily detritus. They will soon enough come kicking and screaming to embrace recrimination.

Toughness and tautness of mental attitude when on external display promote situations where capability tends to go brittle when put under internal pressure. Strength of individual character draws energy from inner resources called hidden wells of cosmic energy. Thus pronounced ability is augmented through a sustainability of Living Energy we are advised to simply call Love.

Integration of parts to establish a rhythmic pulse throughout the whole system usually falls short because of certain missing ingredients. We number them as ten. There are many variants to each theme. Tapping into the reservoir of enduring relationship brings about an expanded viewing over future fields we assiduously work to cultivate.

****

Mind and Memory

May 2023

The scattered pieces in memory need to be put together. The missing ingredient is your very own stranger. Peace is formed through merging isolated pieces in mind and memory called fragmentation.

Unnamed: There are two separate coded areas where we are involved in exploring futurity development. One is the mental state of being present in the everyday occurrences and the other is a memory involvement that references the brilliance in essence. With the oncoming arrival of the Fifth Dimension and The Awakening to A New Mind it does not appear there is going to be any major shift or rearrangement in the physicality of the planetary system. Rather, there is to be a rearrangement in mind and realignment in memory to refurbish that which has been referenced as exchanging new lamps for old.

The shifting of interest for human progression appears to be a mental uplifting or upgrading in intelligence quotient; a rearrangement of old patterns into memory accord to suitably meld with the expanding brain size suitable for the new era of Fifth Dimension. We as pioneers are on track with clearing our memory fields to allow a fresh flow of awakened understanding to occupy and enthuse present day brain cells.

That which will be realized is the present daydreaming state that delays mental advancement. Such a temporary setback has a short-lived span. The kicker, if you like, is while humans talk knowledgeably about reality what they do not realize is that the reality they speak of is no more than proportional. When they wake from the half-lived dream state they occupy then there will be the dawning realization of whom they truly represent.

We can move further afield with our cosmic recordings and as new material is fed through to us; we will on feed it for public digestion. We offer those who have the wish or desire to grow in cosmic stature, the availability of gaining a Greater Understanding in Living Free of those loose impediments we call blockages or hurdles that delay the opportunity for futurity growth. A rearrangement of the present day mental illusionary practices makes available new arrangement opportunities for entangled memories deadlocked in the psyche vaults.

Aria: It is a matter of shifting the settings to access the new memories or those that are already there.

Unnamed: Yes. Clearing away old wasted and distorted memories allows a fresh set of cosmic memories to surface. Those memories are held in the deep wells of the unconscious will move into the subconscious. Then the subconscious areas of abstracted energy will come bubbling to the conscious surface in everyday minds.

Aria: The mind that we are operating with today is not able to process or express those memories because it was not built to handle them.

Unnamed: The everyday mind has been built to handle most of that which is ongoing daily, but it is clogged or overloaded with planetary garbage we nominate as detritus.

Aria: So the mind is having an upgrade in memory recall. Is that what you are saying?

Unnamed: I was reading an item here today: they have discovered an ancient mosaic in Palestine territory in central Gaza that is a replica of some palace tiling in a courtyard dating back thousands of years. A farmer decided to plant an olive tree in his backyard and the shovel scraped against something hard. He called his son and they dug for weeks. They have uncovered this huge mosaic of marble flooring in beautiful condition. They are suggesting it dates from the Byzantine era.

Aria: What you are saying is that history is gradually re-surfacing to give us more of the human story, because in present day mindfulness we only carry a small portion of the story.

****

The Hard Yards in Building a Greater Understanding

Each human system sustains two separated selves that have been described poetically as mind and heart, body and soul. We list their availability for the purpose of Greater Understanding as presence and essence. In exercising a variety of living standards, our consideration is designed to return adverse layers of duality estrangement into one completed core energy. Each of us, nominated as a cosmic pioneer working for futurity benefit of communal welfare, is allotted different areas of work to achieve certain results regarding the patterning of human life; we are, firstly, to achieve a balanced agreement within ourselves and then, and only then, an allotted understanding of being one to exchange with like-minded others.

The hard yards of mind development on offer are not that difficult for those prepared to engage in shared acts of willingness to achieve a mutual progression. Building a solid support foundation is on offer so the perceptive mind can attain and maintain balance and clarity on an individual basis wherever it encounters disputed areas of human discord locked in memory.

Depthing or digging through planetary levels of consciousness is a necessary requirement to ensure a solid base for a futurity building formation. Then ask why do people not employ similar methods of personal digging and diving mentally to establish a sound foundation of common understanding, one that will forge mental security in balanced behaviour and develop a more distinguished order of discipline within their developing character?

We state our competence clearly to provide simple guidelines for acquiring new levels of intelligent understanding. These new levels promote improved health, an enrichment of provisioned wealth in Greater Understanding, and an enjoining process in personal relationships that will endure the ravages of present day living concerns. These benefits attain to advanced levels in mind and memory that are not available on the open markets of education facilities today. Nor do we intend in the early stages of production to make it so.

We are about sharing with interested people a fresh product of mind expansion, providing a stable base with an accompanying and all-encompassing vision of future practice. The modules we have prepared can relate this newly derived information into simple formats for practical use on a global basis. We offer this advanced information on an exchange basis to those who desire new methods of Living Free of mental/emotional pressure.

There is a New Day arriving, a New Life filled with delightful expression, without the cloistered stagnation of drug-ridden dependency so prevalent in modern society.

****

Many Books I have Read

Many books have I read
Many paths I've been led
To seek the eternal truth
And I've heard people say
This or that is the way
Set in their illusions of proof

They told me of a god
Who gave the devil a prod
Working to enact humility
Some spoke of the lame
Whom they seemed to blame
For losing sight of eternity

Each one as they prayed
Lay on a bed they had made
Of faults and fears from belief
They were caught in their pride
No matter how hard they tried
Lies offered only temporary relief

When my footsteps had turned
The one thing I had learned
That nothing existed above
Nor below for that matter
While inane religious chatter
Diminishes the feeling of Love

Though Love is around
It is not so easily found
Where should one start to begin
Reality thought is quite unfair
When Love is not out there
The search has to start within.

Chapter VI

Greater Energy

Unnamed One: *We who are Unnamed, know the steps that are to be taken. We are of the tree whose boughs are unshaken. We know thee, your strengths, and your weaknesses. We love thee without reason. Simply put, it is because we acknowledge your purpose.*

Love Absorbs All

14th December 2015

Lucifer speaks on behalf of the Great Mother energy.

Lucifer: It is interesting to understand that the inner and the innate self are just as competent to argue for their area as the ego pretence. What that means is that the ego self was universally built because were it to be coming from the beyond dimensions as we understand energy, there would be no cause for argument. These are dimensional areas or levels, and in the returning back home, which is Love absorption, we each have to traverse those gradients of soul.

Xan: Who is in charge?

Lucifer: The way Lucifer sees it, we are caught or compelled to play in whatever zone or area where we are operating. In the zone of the cosmic, we could say that the seven sisters, the Pleiades, are somewhat in charge, because they have a control and a inclusive of planet Earth. It is a commitment that goes beyond the solar self. No doubt at some stage the sisters or some of the sisters will come in to collaborate.

Xan: They have already come in.

Awakening to Living Energy

Lucifer: Yes, but they came in to show us their previous life style. Let us see them come in to speak with us on their more advanced understanding for futurity benefit.

Let us say that Lucifer has not given up on his Aunties. He appreciates their past and the painful lessons they went through. He also sees that in their over viewing situation of planet Earth and its people that for them there is a new dawn of awakening also, and that energy form can be passed on or through the people of planet Earth.

The people who are subject to the seven sisters' involvement still have not run the gambit of the seven deadly sins. By that, I mean that they have not cleared themselves of the influence of those disruptive, let us call them corrupt, positions that the sisters found themselves absorbed in countering.

What each of us has to come to terms with is that the planetary body we occupy is caught in the third dimensional energy zone. Our role, in advising of the Greater Understanding of Love energy, is that we are to move outside planetary discord, which lacks the benefit of communal accord.

Xan: Explain that.

Lucifer: Our future benefit is involved in enjoinment with others: the promotion of joy, the idea of pleasure, the acceptance of being specifically assigned, or what some people call uniqueness, is not and never was available to reach planetary fruition. What is available when we are prepared to apply ourselves to the interlinking of what is pain, what is pressure, and then what becomes achievable in that which we call an enjoinment of selves. When we can reach that developmental stage of sharing and caring within, then we have completed a circuit.

Lucifer once more wants to make clear that he endorses the movement of little children. His role of bringing into substantiation the beauty that is Truth is the understanding that we, in coming together as one, bond with the totality of energy that we call All.

When we break or boil down everything that we are involved in, we will eventually realize that there is no imagined adversary state, which can outclass the understanding that we are Love-in-Being. In that understanding, we are beyond the planetary substitution for Intelligence growth classified as knowledge. However, in the meantime, until people reach for that greater level of comprehension, cosmic Intelligence is our necessary passage for exploration.

We cannot reinforce it more that Love is our very foundation. That Love is All. Love does not divide or separate, that Love is both conclusive and

Greater Energy

inclusive. Love is the enjoinment of all the areas that have felt the pain of separation. Love absorbs everything. In closing areas of dislocation, Love embraces all.

We remind each of us that we are the children of the Great Mother. Our work on this planet and the flight of Greater Understanding that is to flow throughout the cosmos, demonstrates All is Love.

We remind each of us that we are Love-in-Being. No attempts to deny that situation can remove us from who we are and what we are to contribute into the greater energy that will shift this third dimensional planet into Fifth Dimensional futurity. We were born anew to promote the greater energy of Intelligence and Love. We will make sure that our required essence of enjoinment is what we process into the Fifth Dimension.

It is not male energy that will introduce into the cosmic system a new level of classic integration. It is the beauty of integrated cosmic understanding, which brings into being the future enjoinment of human development. This is where we are to move into the fresh and more beautiful formation of Greater Understanding.

The human species are a special creative form of entity that has been deliberately built to bring Love energy into personal being. The structure of the foreseeable programmed development is not fully established yet. Humans, as we understand their present configurations, lack the necessary drive for completion. Humans as we understand the overview are frigid. They do not have the competency or the capability of opening themselves to engage a level of beauty that is presently beyond human comprehension.

They are devoid of appreciating joy located within being. They are devoid of reciprocating Love energy. What they are part of is an ongoing argument. What they are part of are chords of disagreement. What they are part of today is lacking an arraignment of future harmony, a deliverance of a greater arrangement, which offers an understanding of living purpose that is beyond planetary pain and pressure.

The incoming levels we speak of are beyond the present-day areas involving human matters. We are representative of those who are beyond memory. We are required to be involved in sorting through and demonstrating the inclusion of Love energy into the awakening memories of the human species.

****

Discussion with the WE Energy

Cosmic Entity/Energy

09th November 2015

WE Energy: The human idea of death is nonsensical. It has no living understanding. It has no basis for realization. It has no foundation offering the Greater Understanding of Life that WE who are beyond memory are involved in demonstrating into planetary and cosmic tuition.

Our work has formulated through recent times. Previously WE had to hold back. WE had to sustain our understanding, but were not allowed to promote Life as the Living Energy. The idea of life in the planetary sense stems from a perception of death. All of your religious leaders today will insist that the future of human life is death.

On the other hand, our understanding of human life is an instituted understanding of future development: WE endorse Love. WE promote Intelligence as the Greater Understanding and WE will tell human ministry…ministry is the word that comes to mind…though we do not use it in any religious sense…the ministry of human mentality that their future is assured. The weaknesses they abjure at this time is a temporary hiccup in their advancement of Greater Understanding, which we nominate as Intelligence.

Life cannot be locked down. It cannot be named or nominated or be somebody's plaything. We say that Life is meant to be realized. WE say that Life is Love personified. In each one of us when we can realize that we are more than what planetary life can offer we become part of a Living Energy structuring that is beyond universal.

The 'you' of the universal order holds back advancement. The Love and Intelligence that we can offer the living instrumentality is missing in human consequence. People think when they buy the story that they are unique then as such, their instrumentality is greater than the cosmic surrounds. They are locked down because that idea gives the cosmic surrounds a greater advantage. That is paradox. And WE say to those who are prepared to have their minds opened that the cosmic levels are a barrier towards them understanding their linkage with the greater beyond.

That is why we say to you, when the first ball is tossed to you, hit it; if you do not, from then on, you are compelled to hit out without the benefit of the initial strike. In other words if you are offered the opportunity to strike out for Home, take it. Do not second-guess; second-guessing will not bring you Home. That is it for the evening, folks.

We Who are Beyond Memory – Beyond the Human Idea

03rd February 2016

WE Energy: As far as Lucifer understands the work we are involved in simply means we are to progress beyond the human idea that they have in hand the fundamental understanding of Truth. We who are beyond memory state clearly that Truth is not available to those who consider that they have a call on living components.

People may think that they are entitled to call the shots. The Greater Energy declares and demonstrates such thinking is iconic and ironic. It cannot offer a greater level of commensurate understanding. It is a waste of useless conjecture to consider such capability is available for human purpose.

That which demonstrates Wisdom, Beauty, Style, and Grace comes from a Greater Understanding that underlines female deliverance. That which demonstrates Truth, Unity, and Equality, comes from deliverance that co-ordinates human balance, which no longer is subject to chords of disharmony because of cosmic arguments.

Luxor: So it is for us who sit around this table to locate a construction of discriminating patterns that offer life enjoinment. We are to put into the everyday disturbed areas of weakened argument a remedial tonic in mind and memory that fortifies the benefit of Greater Understanding.

****

The Unnamed Ones

8th December 2021

A cosmic message received from the Unnamed Ones.

Luxor Mack and Jézel are just two of many advocates we use to convey cosmic messages to humanity. In planetary language, we will join in wishing Luxor a happy birthday. We will also take the opportunity to advise people to start using the word community in place of outworn framed versions of society.

The people of this world are not in cosmic jeopardy. What is being replaced is the third and fourth dimensional effects with a more enlightened atmosphere that is cosmically relayed. Bearing that in mind, we recommend that people shift their spotlight from constantly playing on the human presence, to give more consideration to the cosmic essence nominated as the energy within.

Awakening to Living Energy

We would call it transference of interest. As we have worked with introducing trance-formation for elucidation, the next step indicates transference from the interest in body formation to illuminate the intention of soul energy kick-starting new cosmic growth in global humanity.

****

The Embrace of the Beloved Mother – Oneness

In my dream I felt a hand on my arm
Realized the hand was of my Beloved One
Therefore, I placed my hand over its hand
As bidden my body started to open
Slowly, then more rapidly
I began tumbling as well as spinning
It was as though I were in a giant womb
Soft, warm and darkly fecund
A feeling of joy spread through me
Like the taste of warm honey
I woke with an understanding
My dream was of me
Embraced by ME
Eternally One.

No Ritual

The embrace of the Beloved cannot be experienced through desire or longings for immortality. Only through acceptance is the energy of ME warranted as greater than planetary will or choice. With the merging into the greater energy, the feeling of belonging, the understanding of coming Home can be achieved, and thus realized as we are one.

There is no ritual of worshipping to be followed. No dramatics. No ceremony to perform. Certainly, there is no tradition. In acceptance, there is nowhere left to go and very few to share the Greater Understanding of Life experienced on a planetary level. Aloneness, not loneliness is a prelude to the awakening of whom each of us represents. We are one and the same in the eyes of Greater Energy.

We are able to waken to a stillness and veritable silence that deafens the outer senses. Should we seek the music of the spheres, it is there in accord with the Angel singing. Conversations covering a range of cosmic matters of interest are available. What can any planetary existence offer to replace the delights of sharing a Greater Understanding of Life and Living Free with the Great Mother and The One who are the cosmic givers of life?

****

Chapter VII

New Millennium

The Unnamed One: *Be advised that institutionalized practices in society are in disarray and will continue to crumble until they are suitably rearranged to register a firm foundation in communal welfare. A New Day is appearing, but there are still chaotic events ahead that at the moment spell incoming waves of disaster. Unless there are enough people throughout the world today, ready to settle the traumatic unrest first within their being and then as a sign of genuine friendship by offering a helping hand to support others less fortunate.*

The False Dawn of 2000

The new millennium has begun well and truly. Yet the human mind is still besieged and embattled with past memories that have built a fortress mentality of ego suppression to maintain an artificial grossness of planetary standards lacking foundation. People are bound up in crass belief patterns framed from recurring ideas that invariably lack the potential for futurity growth.

The new age dawning came and went in early 2000 like a false sprite of spring that offered much in anticipation and rendered very little value in substance. Like a precocious child, it showed its tongue to a waiting world and then left to play its illusionary games of mock belief elsewhere.

Today the collective world mind is being thrown back onto its own resources in finding new forms of resilience to climactic disasters and viral infections. People have tried different forms of religious faith in an attempt to find some awakening benefit through practising various degrees of spirituality. Societies have worked at building scientific knowledge and have become so enamoured by the outer scaffolding of presumed reality built to please the eye that they have lost sight of the internal structuring of being that offers wisdom and beauty.

Awakening to Living Energy

The internal beauty and strength demonstrated in being one in wholeness was never a considered option for scientific discovery to pursue. The left portion of the mind and brain relies on external stimuli to reinforce its dominant programming of ego constraint, which is incapable of admitting structural weaknesses located in its varied and maladjusted systems of mind and brain. Now is the time for the bell of cosmic changes to be rung. Because they were not told, what people have not learnt is that the ringing requires to be led by the resounding bell tones of Wholeness, the big W, that which stands for completion. Clinging onto the 'I am pretence' professing ego constraints as a glamorous central base in mind is repetitive nonsense and an exercise in futility.

The hallowed halls of social knowledge called resourcefulness in education have sealed their doors and barred their windows against intrusive thoughts of Intelligence that can bring more to understanding circumstances in life than what professional lecturers are presently overpaid to offer society.

Enter stage right the cosmic players dedicated to advancing themes of both Love and Intelligence. They bring a melody from distant memories situated deep within the human psyche. They carry stories that are a portion of the eventual revealing of human heritage. They state clearly that the theories of Darwinism made circus monkeys out of anthropologists. That immortality is a dream born of a frustrated and demented symbolism that torments and tortures those who are obsessed by the greedy awards of an acquisitive mind. What is devotedly referenced as freedom is one more set of chains designed to capture and bind tight the human spirit.

There is so much distorted material that is believed because it was stated and repeatedly related by father figures professing authority, yet what has been circulated carries no relevance to ascertaining whom human entities truly are, where they initially formed from and where they are intent on returning in the immediate future.

Now the veils of ignorance are being removed from the eyes of many and, inevitably, so the height of arrogance and superiority in ego derangement encapsulated by society leaders will be downgraded; statuesque icons of superiority set in mental framing are soon to be toppled. As instigated by divine energy, the measured scales signifying equality will balance and the work of merging the two frames of duality into oneness will be seen to be conclusive.

Forget any notions of this fresh material are rehashes of planetary religions or spiritual new versions of age-old junk. The campaign for realizing Greater Understanding in mind and memory is cosmic in context covering a revamping of science, religions, the interpretation of past and future historic events, as well as educational opportunities for people to make valid connections available within their dual selves. The Fifth Dimension will move people out of their presently held dogmatic situations in cloistered minds that continuously recycle exhausted material from past events.

At present societies in play are cosmically over-viewed as planetary swamps of indulged misinformation that causes Angel energy to label Earth as the planet of lies. The problem is not going to be so much the ability to field questions relating to human and cosmic understandings, as to whether the modern prelates in their chosen fields of authority have either the capacity in mind or the intestinal fortitude to formulate necessary questions of pertinent worth pertaining to futurity stages of personal development.

The cosmic entity-energies we interact with have the ability to scan anyone planetary by the mere mention of their name and thus give us a brief print out according to their present capability and unwavering reliability.

****

Interesting People

We are in agreement with the ending of linear recorded times as they relate to the conclusion of an outdated chapter in the movements of planet Earth and its people into the oncoming Fifth Dimension. The errors maintained in rational thinking, and timing are the reliance on scientific thought crediting linear time and space as distinctive planetary issues governing the lives of people.

Time and space cover a temporary phase in mind and memory only and are subject to cosmic clock influences that are sequentially ordered. Sequential means that something will occur at an appropriately given time and ordered where human controls may appear to influence some events like planetary warming; yet the overall result is cosmically programmed, thus predetermined, and placed in a slotted area for further development. The certainty of shifting patterns to eventuate will happen because of previously set programs that operate beyond the dreaming states of human choice or freewill.

Cosmic influences manifest sequentially. Obvious examples of cosmic timing can be given with respect to the consistent human pulse beat, spontaneous breathing, birthing, puberty, maturity and subsequently timeless energy lifting off the planetary surface.

Awakening to Living Energy

On a greater scale the movement of planets, star systems and galactic order in general can be seen as influenced by the tick-tocking of the sequential clock. What is it that has set the clock a-ticking for planet Earth and its creatures to depart the third dimension? It is called the programmed patterns of the Divine Plan. It is administered in this solar system by Angels and Ancients, elementals, and a Divine Family of four, all who work willingly on behalf of Greater Energy.

Only the ignorance of the rational mind, under the controlling influence of ego management, is scornful of the existence of a greater unnamed essence that absorbs and manages all manner of things, including the paucity of human effort.

Now that the false prophets of the New Age movement have folded their tents, the messengers of cosmic influence move amongst the people in a regulated manner that does not excite or warm the material hearts and emotions of the greedy children occupying the planet. The fingers are to be prised off the jar of peanuts that the simulated monkeys of material status value so much. The egos, like puffed up balloons of hot air, are being further inflated so they are easier to prick and burst asunder. The washing away of egocentricity in thought can be seen as a prelude to the dirty bathwater of beliefs emptying down the gurgler.

What a wonderful language for precise expression is English prose. So many opportunities for analogies that lead into the understanding of never ending paradox. This in turn offers the opportunities for doorways to exit from out of the rational box of ego stricture into the extended vision of an expansive New Mind wakening.

These communications we carry are a cosmic offer to exchange advanced information with people involved in commerce, medical science, religion, sport, education, media and other distinctive areas, who wish for a participatory interest in the development of the next level of mind consciousness. This material is presently stored within the volatile human system nominated as psyche.

We nominate the projected level for human advancement as becoming cosmic, more particularly referenced for planet Earth and creatures as the Fifth Dimension, encompassing and surpassing, the dualistic methods still operative on the planet in these failing twilight times. These present day operations destructing societal values are shortly bound for a mental collapse because the eggs of opportunism, acquisitiveness, and possessiveness are destined for a massive restructuring exercise.

Given there are more than half a million interesting people seeded on the planet, they will come to share their observations in releasing local, national, and international fears and concerns that lack basic foundation. Their role is to first understand and then collapse the ensuing and ongoing rifts in social behaviours prevalent within their disadvantaged and argumentative communities.

The problems in societal waste are to be revealed, understood and addressed for the necessary breakthroughs in communal affairs to occur. There are many ways through the dilemmas facing humanity that are not being considered by the lacklustre controllers of society values.

As a cosmic presentation, we are prepared to offer understandings that will fill many of the present holes of futile and wasted effort employed today. To enable that to happen there is a requirement for dialogue between those who continue to spread denial and those who are competent to understand there is a Living Energy emanating Beauty and Wisdom, now available and waiting to be accessed internally. This Living Energy of Love extends far beyond what ego management presently dictates as value.

Consider the need for appropriate human responses to overbearing disasters soon to plague the planet where unwitting people are being caught up in cycles of despair.

****

2K Bug

Prophecies written by Luxor in 1999

The year 2K bug or virus carries the demand or insistence for each person to move out of the penned derangement of herd mentality to develop their own particular individual style for progression. Pressure will be heavy on intimate relationships where the future requirement is for each person to stand in their own light as a gifted right.

Not that people can own the light. The light is cosmic. The right relates to their given or gifted space, which is a proportional sharing of the light. Human societies have only paid lip service to the requirements of individual character.

The pigs of society, the autocratic controllers, have manipulated democratic procedures for their own benefit for far too long. These pigs of swill will become bogged down by wallowing in their own mucking mud. They have used and abused the energy of other creature forms for so long they are incapable of supporting themselves. Money will not buy the necessities of Living Free from mental pain in the early quarter of the new millennium. Therefore, self-esteem as a support system for a faltering ego phase will be at a loss to stand and will slowly dissipate as an asset. No one can buy individual worth.

Morals will come to be seen as a part of the web of illusionary entrapment amid other delusions of heavenly grandeur endorsed by the crafty minds of the self-appointed righteous. The hierarchies developed morals as controlling patterns for the masses and religious based societies, albeit tribal, still want to maintain their rigidity using torture, murder and warfare in greater or lesser degrees. There is the oft-repeated suggestion or claim that moral standards maintain the spirit of goodness. Morals have never been instrumental in developing a falsity of goodness because any form of control inhibits the demonstration of innate feelings, which align with joyful expressions of worth.

The national superpowers of the western world that have stood four square for democracy, morals, ethics and all things bright and beautiful have never delivered stability to the people in the country jurisdictions they control. Where are their dreams situated today? They are lost in the turmoil of maintaining the roles of global police enforcement to dominate populations foreign and local so their monetary systems can maintain a superior status in world markets.

What they have done as a rebound is deny individual status in their societies. Equality was so proudly defended as self evident in their early platforms of constitutional power. Today the words carry a hollow sound, a distant mockery echoing inside de-mock-racy and is certainly not evident today. It will be even less so with the calamitous breaking apart of ever-nearing future planetary events that are beyond the pale of human control.

The rueful use of 'self-evident' in planetary terms means much the same as people creating their own realities; to use the verbiage of new age parlance.

****

On Human Foundation

Planetary science can never equate its findings to align with Truth. Nor can visual works of copied art bestow beauty on the beautiful. Greeks in the age of Plato and thereabout times did their best or damnedest to define love, truth, beauty and goodness by separating each into what they considered were elementary components. Their attempts failed miserably then and, because philosophers, psychologists and sociologists of today peddle the same material from those same age old premises, humans are still being deprived of a birthright in Greater Understanding, which opens the individual mind to realize a destined purpose enclosed within the authentic being.

Science has built its half-baked premises on measurement of quantities; now it is bound and bowed down by its owning frames of restrictive qualifications. This parody of false values compulsively propels the exponents of the various professions into uttering indifferent forms of exaggerated nonsense. The scientific minds that initially set the limiting boundaries that would control human thinking in society were not able to visualise a surrounding cosmos, boundless in energy beyond time and space.

Any prisoner with a conditioned mental re-flux called memory may have an image of what is considered freedom. What has been responsively imposed on human memory has no true sense of direction or expansion and therefore is not aligned with the cosmic understanding of Life and Living Free. The illusion of correctness, the staged stances by those in positions of superiority insisting on having futurity projections mocked, is no more than smoke and mirrors set in place to bewilder the minds of the many who audaciously seek explanations to pacify their deliberately deranged thought processes.

Cosmic understanding of Life and Living bewilders, in the main, the spruikers for the moral majority and those that seek understanding from studying the scattered grains of sand deemed to be the last word in certified knowledge. Science has fixated on becoming the imagery of stars and has never dreamed of researching and realising the immensity of hidden meaning contained within the hidden psyche. The seduction of material knowledge has euchred indiscernibility and blurred credibility of the inner-self. What is also immeasurable and unthinkable in scientific parlance is the promise of A New Day and the shift of the planet and its creatures into another dimension nominated as the Fifth.

****

The Future of Human Kind

How are we to locate balance in our lives to dispel the anger and irritations forming from mental frustration? When is the unification of two apportioned selves to occur? Why is humankind in general at a loss in locating the simplest of answers to posited questions? When will a Greater Understanding of Life and Living Free be made apparent for the communal benefit of all?

The learned ones, philosophers and mystics, past and present, have predicted that the species of humankind is experiencing 'the ending of recorded time.' Can people ignore these predictions because the sun still shines on the everyday scenarios? Are we capable of alternating time and space to ensure there is a smooth evolutionary process of movement from past to present to future developments?

Humankind is at the precinct of a glorious future. Who is prepared to involve their selves in a previewing of destiny we call futurity? Who is prepared to knock to see if the promised door to a new life will magically be thrown open? Who is gifted with ears to hear, and eyes to see the remaking and rewarding benefits of human destiny?

When the eyes of awakening people are fully opened, they will plainly see it is the bigots in society who speak loudly and falsely in accusing others of chicanery. It is those wearing blackened hearts who talk loudly of opposing evil and besting moral enemies, thus urging the mindless society dwellers to endorse their actions in maintaining senseless warfare between nations.

It is those who declare themselves righteous in daily prayers who have often the dirtiest of secrets to hide. In the oncoming days of reckoning, people such as these will certainly scatter and run in states of confusion. But where can they possibly hide?

****

Spirituality and New Age

Spirituality is a planetary concept acknowledging there is a Greater Energy.

New Age attempts to find Wisdom, quantify life as being of three parts, body, mind, and spirit.

As such, those who opted for spirituality in practice could not help but quantify what they saw as repressive life outwardly. In return, though sometimes building towards a broader view of various happenings, they still subject them to be enclosed in universal boundaries limiting mental expression. These lockdown areas present gross barriers their planetary minds cannot surpass.

What that suggests is that people have habitually measured cloth according to its cut. Put another way it means they continued to copy and practise crass material taken either from what they had read, observed, or at some time may have heard recounted.

Therefore, they took onboard as being gospel, whatever was offering as grist for the mill, or at least seen as valued truths, to be emulated spiritually with the added advantage in mind ascension. Advantages taken on or into spiritual values are one of the reasons that new age activity whenever introduced on the planet has such a shortened span of artificial life.

Spiritualism as practised is a planetary dreaming state with very little sustainable energy.

****

Vitality and New Life

What is promoted as vitality?

Vitality as energy within being stimulates the nerve centres in the brain for creative and thoughtful mind expansion through determining physical expression. Vitality opens the unrealized chakra points. Vitality is fertile energy abstracted from the deep wells of soul. It comes as a breakthrough measure when releasing wasted excrement in mind and memory.

It is known by many names, which at best describe aspects of it and cannot encompass the whole. Only the energy that we have experienced can be known and shown, a stillness, which is within us and without is moving.

Those of us with innate courage to progress are waking and clearing our minds of residue; a new energy is starting to flow through our systems. For the want of a more encompassing word, we call it vitality.

How is it realized in mind? By letting go of waste material, we nominate as detritus.

Let go of old beliefs, conditioned thought patterns that do not work for you. One day we must face our mirrored selves without the imagery of a persona that is masked.

Anxieties, fear based doubts, are meant to be worked through and released, not stifled by the use of patented drugs, for where they are suppressed they split into many more fragmented pieces.

Humanity is being called upon to place religions behind them. What is true within being cannot be lost. Only the dead wood of old habits, beliefs, and superstitions are to be released. Allow them to go back to where they can be collapsed and renewed. They are manmade obstacles. Only the teachings of advanced understanding in worth stand fresh and vital.

What of the new tutors?

They stand, steady and true, ready to work with you. Religions tell you there are no new tutors and would lock you up in old ways of ritual and superstition. The new tutors are standing by. Those that hear the inner call to return Home will respond. Unity of cause has already been achieved. Humanity is the effect.

The New Day is dawning clear. New Life means fresh purpose in Living Free.

****

The Kingdom of Heaven

The Kingdom of Heaven was an overused term 2000 years ago to signify a cosmic plane of rapture, an ecstatic existence that today is more generally referenced as a return to Home. To view it as some form of beatific after-life is an error in calculation caused by the centralized presence of planetary ego. Home is a beyond dimensional state with a much more refined vibrational level than what presently exists for humans on this third level of dimension.

The Angels describe Home as the core of being. The memory of its influence on future purpose lies dormant within the singularity of each persona, awaiting the individual status of growth to make its appearance within being.

****

The End of a Period of Time

The year of the millennium 2000 came and went without any great fanfare or flourish. The fears of the religious and superstitious populations were heightened and then allayed when the world remained in orbit and the sun still rose and set to the timed perceptions of their egocentric minds. For the members of formulated religions god had answered their prayers for a continuance of planetary survival.

The sceptics who doubted the advent of biblical revelation could now take the bed-covers off their faces and say with some sighing of relief, 'We told you so'. The scientists once more could demand excessive funding to reach for the stars while millions of people starve for the need of scientific and financial assistance to sustain their finite worlds of scant necessity.

The Angels do not consider humans as stupid because such labelling would be a biased approach towards a naivety in living built from eons of planetary ignorance. The rational mind as well as the part of the Neo-cortex brain that functions on local memory by relying on book knowledge, are no more than carriers of available material extremely limited in scoping detail.

Minds that have not been trained to receive internal messages of Greater Understanding are incapable of processing cosmic data when delivered. In the world of the rational mind that uses the human eye to physically see outwardly there are deliberate distortions set in place that is meant to confuse the sensibilities of the unwitting viewers of daily events. At its most expansive vision, the view is only proportional in its limited capacity of shared sensory intake.

****

Lucifer's take on New Age Hype

So many people in western societies were treated to new age hype about the Aquarian beginnings of the year 2000. There were so many false prophets, pundits and devotees of self-proclaimed masters busily channelling Ascended Masters, Archangel Michael, Sai Baba, plus the remnants of Melchizedek energy reflecting Atlantis glory and ultimate destruction.

There were others who wrote of speaking personally with God and sundry type Angels who had the power to selectively heal measles, mumps and other such childhood ailments. They offered vain hopes for a gullible humanity with the need for protection by taking care to ward off psychic attacks from the people of darkness operative in the spirit worlds.

The idea of the new millennium carried with it vague feelings of foreboding brought on by religious prophecies of end times. The revelations spoke of Armageddon where the armies of the righteous ones of god would wrestle with the might of the Great Dragon energy and in winning the fight for the righteous a new world would dawn with the triumphant certainty of a thousand years of peaceful activity for the victorious.

When the sun continued to shine, with computers and electricity still operative, the nascent expectations of less than exciting times slumped and most people settled back after the celebrations of another new year into the ho-hum boredom of the business world progressing as usual.

A Moving Day Expanding Love

Fear becomes a closer ally when we
Cease to regard pain as the enemy
As a teacher trained in Love is loath
To see fear a necessary part of growth
Fear disappears when we learn our lessons
Viscous pain accrues to protect possessions

Love allows freeness of expression
Through not seeking vain possession
Nor presuming to get in the way
When we bruise by having our day
Or being persistent in wanting a say
Invariably stumble and cruel the play

Love seeks no altering of condition
When mind traps move into position
Fools bent on errands will never know
What remains as what and why that is so
Ploy changing to seek unconditional love
Separates further lines from above

What delivers a limiting presence
Thus denying the purity of essence
It matters not what some say or do
Truth reveals where hearts are true
Love eternally stands clear as it is
Requiring no further superlatives.

Chapter VIII

Legacy

The Unnamed One: *The Angels say there is a new world that is coming upon us and it is coming fast.*

Futurity Benefit

We acknowledge the quality of cosmic energy we carry within our being and we work to realize the unified harmony demonstrated in togetherness.

As representatives of The Unnamed and Greater Energy, we have visited this planet many times before over a period of two and a half million in linear years. This time on departure we will leave a legacy of Love, Truth and Intelligence as a significant benefit for further human development we call futurity.

When we lift off one last time, we will leave behind a blueprint for human performance that will benefit communal arrangements befitting the Fifth Dimension.

****

Discussion with an Angel

07th June 2018

Angel: Good evening. The world is too much with us. What that means is that the conversation has become too serious. The repercussions of lighthearted banter hardly make it worthwhile. The quote goes, 'become as children'. So let the woes of those around us flutter into the waves that reach the shore and die a natural death. Do not allow them to go back into the ocean and gather strength once more.

We have never asked that you compare yourselves with each other, nor that you are found wanting either yourself or others around, nor lacking in certain features that you don't enjoy. So let us become less serious about that which is a serious matter. Otherwise, you will find cracks appear unnecessarily because of the pressure that is placed upon you by yourself and others that by some strange definition, you are required to become super-humans. You have never been asked to be super-humans.

Come to that, you have never asked to be human in features. We are talking about emotional features that are not able to be avoidable and therefore the case has been for each of you to divest yourself of the systems of belief, of the mindsets through which you have seen the world. Allow that to dissolve so that emotional conflicts are allowed to settle and disappear into the mists and let the Little People take care of that.

So we do not ask you to gouge out each other's eyes because one, you are having a bad day or two, or that you consider another has not been given enough prods to deliver the goods. And what goods are they? You are only second-guessing. We have never asked you to second-guess.

And if you consider we are asking something of you, you are incorrect. We do not want you to do anything special. In some ways you need to give yourselves a leave pass. This is not a human exercise where you are either rewarded or punished because you have ticked certain boxes or corrected some that have been crossed. We must reiterate once more - that is not how the Greater Energy operates.

The shift into the Fifth Dimension will happen. You do not have to make it happen. You do not have to press any buttons so that the humans will automatically enjoin with you. We have told you on more than one occasion that humans in the present will not enjoin with you save a few, a small few. Nor the next generation, save a few. However, you are to leave a legacy for the following generation. You are to leave footsteps of a profound nature through the recovery of certain items so that you can go into the discovery of who you are.

That is the legacy.

That is the program.

We have also told you that the items that you are putting forward today into various media outlets will cause a small furore and it may introduce a few people into the arena. We have never asked that you bring in the crowds.

Legacy

Have we said before that you are guinea pigs? Have we said before that you are working through your items so that we can see what is occurring, the production thereof, and the influences thereof? We never asked you to be worldwide provocateurs. We have asked for you to shine your light. For that to occur, firstly you need to move, into the shadows and clear the cobwebs so that your light may shine and shine brightly. Moreover, were the grouping as a whole to do that exercise then there the influence can spread across the planet and yes, that will assist people into the Fifth Dimension.

Nevertheless, let us again reiterate, the Fifth Dimension is on its way. No one, nobody will arrest its motion. Therefore, if you have in your heads that you are bigger than Ben Hur then remove it immediately. It is the energy that is paramount. Beautiful! Not able to be compared with, described, or talked about. While you are in your small minds, it is beyond your comprehension. We call the mind on this planet small because it is enclosed in a tiny space, enclosed for safety purposes.

Let us reiterate once more. None of you here is a human. You are enclosed in a human body. You inhabit a third dimensional space. You have taken on the co-ordinates of the human and the reactions thereof. Yet you are not human. That must say one or two things. One, obviously aspects of human existence you still like well enough to continue with. Moreover, when we talk of that we talk of clinging to beliefs and emotional reactions around being human.

We are not asking you to avoid any activity whatsoever on this planet. Merely that you be aware that it is a human attitude stemming from beliefs and moving into emotional shit. What a more joyous place this were to be, if you allowed others in this grouping to be.

If that is not enough for the Greater Energy, the Greater Energy will be required to intervene. Spend the next few days talking about likenesses. Build them up, bring them forward. Bring lightness into your conversation. We have not asked you to have a death as in a death on occasions when you are enjoining with each other. Bring out the laughter, bring out the jokes and see what happens next.

This world, it will evolve, it will move, and it will turn. It is already in process of turning. The third dimensional world is on its way out. You will see that by the obvious nature of that which has been fallow in the soil, rotting away is now being turned over so that it is exposed to the open air and it smells like shit. Because it has been turned over in the oxygenated air, it will eventually clear. Thank you everybody for this evening.

All give their thanks.

****

Another Discussion with an Angel

08th November 2017

After dinner, Jézel moves into channel mode and an Angel speaks on behalf of the Great Mother.

Angel: On this fragile planet, fragile in the sense that it is quite possible that not only will glass break, but egos and mirrors will also break very easily these days. The Love that is sought by humans is not to be found. Because…?

Satania: Because it is not foundation. It is attraction.

Angel: Well yes, people want a certain sense of security.

Xan: Ownership.

Angel: Yes. So the Love that is sought will never be found. Consequently, there is a never-ending sorrow in the human psyche.

Satania: Like a yearning.

Angel: Well, you call it yearning. You would have the yearning, but not everyone has the yearning for the deeper Love. Most still have not reached that state. I would say there are so many surface levels of human conditioning. Yearning is a deeper level.

Most humans live on the surface. Once you embrace the Great Mother there is an endlessness of feeling, adept at understanding that which cannot be necessarily explained, reasoned, and definitely not quantified.

The Mother is not into the numbers game of quantity. The Mother exemplifies the qualities for all those who are capable of seeing. She exemplifies the qualities of Love energy. She shows her face for those who are ready and therefore able to see. And thence incorporate in their being that which is already in Love.

The mind that operates for you on a daily basis is incapable of understanding or seeing, or well beyond being able to feel the vibration that comes from the Great Mother Energy.

So the more you are able to remove yourself from the everyday mind…thank your mind for the everyday…and then suggest quite strongly that you will reside in behind the everyday mind that signifies you will be able to understand more clearly a situation that is before you.

You will be able to sense the inequitable areas inside of the humans that you exchange with. And thence you will be able to see, understand, feel and taste ahead of the exchange with another human…well when I say another human, another person in a human body.

We need to sometimes remind ourselves that that is the case. You are encased in a human body for the purposes of survival on this planet. But you cannot and will not retain this body. It is not yours. Nevertheless, it will serve you for this time around.

Therefore, when you see it like that you will not need to give it such high status. None the less, you are required to look after it so that you can maintain your balance on the planet and thence your connection with the Great Mother and the Greater Energy, which encompasses all.

I ask each of you to absorb all that is before you. On these occasions you may absorb areas of energy that are shady at best. The more that you can do this with equilibrium the more you will stand strong under all circumstances.

Stand tall in the face of hostilities and criticism. Do not block what it is people have to throw at you. You may fall briefly, you may quiver, but eventually you will stand firm.

So yes, I am considered to be called an Angel, who is devoted to the Great Mother; that which resides inside of each of you. So take in the poison arrows of people and from these elements you will grow and you will strengthen for the work that is ahead of you on behalf of the Great Mother Energy.

****

Discussion with Beyond the Beyond

17th June 2014

Lucifer goes into a fit of sneezing, the number counted is nine, which is then followed by a series of hiccups. When he recovers an entity/energy then comes through to speak using Luxor as the medium of exchange with those present.

Beyond the Beyond: Well, Lucifer, you have always wanted to meet with the energies that are greater than those who are directing your future. Well, we are available tonight because we have recognised your dedication to measures beyond normalcy. We credit you with an ability to meet a future that is beyond cosmic understanding. Otherwise, what interest would we have in speaking with you? We are not of the cosmos. We are not even aligned with those that you nominate as beyond the cosmos. We are, as someone has once said, beyond the beyond.

Jézel: We welcome you in.

Beyond the Beyond: And we are happy to share this evening with you. Though there were some who were capable of realising that there was a beyond the beyond, they were not capable of reaching those levels. To Lucifer we grant that elusive understanding. Why? Perhaps it is because Lucifer has never ever settled for second best. Be that as it may, we are happy to introduce Lucifer into the Greater Understanding that is our central core.

When we say this, let us make it clear that you are still working with male intelligence. Though we preceded The Great Mother with our understanding, we do not take away from her the wisdom she brings into life being. However, back to us speaking of our input into planetary and cosmic future.

It was always designated through the Divine Plan that these patterns of greater growth were at some time to become apparent. Though you might say we held back for quite a while because we were not sure the time was suitable or appropriate for the advancement of human understanding.

We have been assured by the work done by Lucifer and Jésu, and, in a smaller way, the compatriots sitting here that the time has come for us to make our understanding clear. This is not for their benefit, but for the benefit of the shift of humans, the planet, and the cosmic areas, all those beings agreeable to a greater life. What can we say except nominate being, because after all is there any other form of life except being?

Can you, any one of you, demonstrate a style of living that is beyond being? If you like, being is in the moment, not in the now. That is one more falsified story that has been used in a planetary sense to confuse humans. You see if you were to acknowledge now, then you would have to deny a past and a future. So now is a lie.

Now does not draw from the energy of the past. It does not allow the benefit of futurity. So we say that now is a lie perpetrated on the human mental faculty. And we say that in tomorrow there is futurity. And we say that in yesterday there was a past. However, we do not use the word now. What we simply use is the word today.

Legacy

Jézel: Would you see it as a continuum of events on an elliptical curve rather than a now?

Beyond the Beyond: *Laughing.* Jésu always loved to throw the curly ones. An elliptical curve?

Jézel: Well, it is a continuum. There is no particular now. There is a continual movement, which if not allocated on a linear level, then it has to be on an elliptical curve.

Beyond the Beyond: And of course the elliptical curve is known as a wave or a...

Jézel: A wave, yes.

Beyond the Beyond: So yes, but we do not see your question of continuum as a necessity for the closeness of this moment.

Jézel: So how does the closeness of the moment differ from what you are saying? Where using the word 'now' is not appropriate, but the closeness of the moment is?

Beyond the Beyond: The closeness of the moment is a shutting down. Closeness means a closing. Tomorrow morning when you awake you will have in front of you a new level of developed understanding. Do not take that lightly. What is now being said to you is as of tonight there is a shutting down of past pressure and pain. Tomorrow when you wake, you will appreciate there is an alleviation of that past pressure. Welcome it.

Jézel: I certainly will welcome it.

Beyond the Beyond: We will not come in very often to speak with you.

Jézel: Have you been nominated before? Have you spoken to us before?

Beyond the Beyond: Lucifer has spoken of us, but perhaps you were not aware.

Jézel: Colour and Sound or beyond that?

Beyond the Beyond: Beyond comprehension. The closest that anyone has ever got to us was the beyond of the beyond.

Jézel: No wonder, Lucifer, you had to sneeze nine times and hiccup several times before the energy could appear.

Beyond the Beyond: *Laughing.* There you go. We are not without our share of friendly amusement. We are not serious in our direction. Well, not fully.

We do take the time out to be amused by the situations that we see occurring in planetary and cosmic areas.

But we can assure you though that we do overview the necessary situations and when it is necessary we will step in to make sure that the future, planetary and cosmic, will follow the appropriate lines that will bring a benefit to the various areas.

With those remarks, we thank you for your attendance to our involvement. And we wish you to know that while you remain on track with the greater energy of Love and Intelligence, we are there to give you the required substance that will bring the joy to fruition that all creatures are deserving of. Thank you again.

Jézel: Thank you very much. *Hugging.*

Satania: Thank you.

Beyond the Beyond: *Kisses her hand.* You are our child.

Xan: Thank you.

Beyond the Beyond: Hey, brother.

****

We Are One

April 2018

Jézel: I don't agree that we are our own masterpieces. We are warped in each other's care. We are part of each other. We are not separate. We are one and we need to come to understand the significance of what that means.

Lucifer: What does it mean to say we are one? It means one energy totally unified in communal purposing beyond human comprehension. Yet as we appear on this planet we are seen as distinctive, separate, singular, part of minority groupings, formed from larger groupings; a portion of a cosmos beyond realization and carrying within our being a miniature styled cosmos of variable types.

We are in the process of merging diffident portions of planetary systems together. As human entities, we have been separated for millions of years from Home and in embracing the light of the New Day the process of mental derangement is reversing. We are in the process of unifying, stabilizing and equalizing. We are bonding in Truth, tantamount to embracing self-realization. We are motivated to be of one mind, one purpose, and moving in one direction. Our work is to assimilate all differences into one conclusive and connective response – namely that we are one.

Each of us, with regard to our own space or territory, is coming from undeveloped areas that wish inclusion in some subliminal manner of advanced understanding. We know that it is only by connection with the Great Mother energy that can realize the destiny for those who require fulfilment. What is fulfilment? It is simply to know that we are bonded as one. Portions of Love were sent forth in many directions, regardless, each was required to aspire towards Greater Understanding. When the All relinquishes a reliance on doubtful meaning called duality, then Love is substantiated.

Lucifer wishes that we develop the understanding that we are all friends, whether we are family, or outside family, an important part of our extended understanding is to acknowledge we are all friends. There is no outer field of consequence to promote argument. There is within each of us the opportune moment to acknowledge joy. When we are realized as one we are no longer separate.

Our role on the planet, which has not yet fully opened, but will shortly occur, is that we are to bring the people on the planet into an all inclusive understanding that we are one. So when people realize we are one with All, who is left standing alone to foster further argument?

****

Notation from the Angels

Love as the proper foundation of living energy.
Through awakening the flame of intelligence
Lay aside the perverse stone that locked away
The next stage or chapter of human endeavour

With the symbolic drawing of the sword
Love dispelled the veil of forgetfulness
To bring to bear the long waited moment
A reunification of the Divine family

With the endorsement of Womanhood
There is recognition of the Mother
As the appropriate hand to knell the old
And give birth to a play of new worlds

She invites the lost children to seek the fire
A return to those who provide acceptance
Pain and fear are removed from past issues
To slip away and dissolve from memory.

Chapter IX

Self-Realizing

The Unnamed One: *Joy and grace are demonstrations in the experience of feeling. We say humans will begin the process of unifying with their inner being of self when they learn to release emotions and once more embrace feelings.*

Unity and Being

We are part of One energy. We are determined as equal and unified. Let go of the idealistic separation in mind and memory and return to embracing wholeness as expressed in unified effort.

That which is demonstrated as energy is One. Only realize the unity contained within self and you become aware of all there is needed to know to grow exponentially. Unity in the mystical sense implies that nothingness exists within being and is beyond stalemated planetary power. Energy referencing Home is the core of being. Anything that is nameable is not accorded the status of being. Names are recorded images that only reflect being and therefore appear to exist as a token reality in some planetary guise or other signifying illusion.

Unification in mind arrives with the knowing that all things set in accord are enjoined as one.

Motto:

WE ARE ONE

We are unified

We are equalized

We are bonded in Truth

Absorbed in Love

Inspired by Intelligence

WE ARE FAMILY.

****

Separation of Parts is Over

Lucifer speaks on the New Day and Love Energy

Divine Mother: *I come not here to give you answers. There is a part inside you that is me and that is you. Love is the essence. It is within and without. Around and about. Above and below. It distils the wine we call Angel juice. Love is available to those who give themselves over. Until today it has lain dormant within the wellsprings of humans. The near future is due time for the cosmic awakening. 2010*

The separation of humans from their divine parentage caused the eruptions of denials and formed the ego belief patterns that resulted in people seeking the iconic worship of gods and goddesses as support systems. That period of illusion is to be no more. The collapse of separation starts with the decline of beliefs that have never carried substance. Without the platform of errant beliefs, the standards maintaining imbalanced societies are no longer valid. The flag bearers for religion and veracity claims in science will be out of work. They are to be replaced by cosmic torchbearers.

Humans are to find wisdom and beauty within their selves. The days of the vain leaders with their false promises of hope and faith leading unto glory will be devastated. Welcome in the dawning of individual status demonstrating worth in wellbeing. Welcome the birthing of a new era where humans will be competent to endorse a Greater Understanding in mind and memory and draw their innate energy from the wells of cosmic resources. It is part of their birthright. Love as immanence is supportive. The imminence of programmed fresh procedures comes with the dawning of the New Day.

****

We are Nothingness

We, who are cosmic in being and as such, only cloaked in human appearance, are aware in this posited state that we know nothing. It is time well spent to absorb and understand clearly that we present as nothing. What then does nothingness represent?

We are to realize that we are emissaries of Love essence, nominated cosmically as Beings-in-Love. There is no reality available on Earth, this so-called planet of responsive lies. Psychosomatic illness is a conditioning of a reluctant mind refusing to acknowledge the developing roots of fresh cosmic growth, so rearrange the outworn patterns of wasted memories and the dreaded pain of the unknown coursing in unsettled minds will disappear. Send out to Angels an invitation to be taken beyond human consciousness, and allow A New Mind to awaken within to greet the workings of A New Day.

Nothingness covers everything in the same way as a blanket of density smothers swards of grass. Clear the mental whiteboard of old planetary material and you will have a suitably vacant space where you are able to write in new levels of worthwhile cosmic understanding. Like lingering areas of detritus, the old wine soured in memory is polluted and must first be emptied harmlessly before fresh wine can be poured into new wine skins.

Thence cometh A New Day, A New Mind, a new vision observing and absorbing renewed articles of vital interest. The detritus of beliefs, superstitions and conditioned responses called lies is wasted old hat material, and required to be emptied or released so wisdom generated from the Great Mother energy arrives unbidden. Do not forget that the guiding hands of Angelcare are with us at all times.

Greater Levels

Our Intelligence and Greater Understanding comes from a long way away and yet it arrives as fresh as moisturised dew on the early morning bed of winter grass. Rearranging of internal patterns in mind and memory cannot be done solely of your own volition. We are meant to share our gifted understandings, so that the information we distribute to others does not come directly from us, rather from the conveyed wishes of the Great Mother.

To reach a greater bonded level in unified Truth we are to merge the two allocated selves, namely soul essence and planetary presence. Ego pretence influencing doubtful minds has held the reins of control for so many years yet no longer carries precedence in the new scale of cosmic awakening. Do not attempt to fight ego in its waning influence. That will only make it stronger. Step away and ask to have a greater system denoting cosmic belonging introduced into your planetary style of living.

We are sometimes mentally confounded when the Angels convey to us our next level of information for Greater Understanding, but grounding new energy to be realized is all about mental balancing. Allow the detritus of discharged beliefs to be replaced with measures of cosmic Intelligence. Be introduced to who you are representing and realize you are not principally human in cosmic stature.

Self Realization

Who you truly are is deemed worthless in planetary terms and as such is beyond planetary price fixing.

What you are contains any amount of toss material, conditioning and superstitious beliefs that maintain wasted mindsets, which are neither valid nor seemly.

People are presently performing in mind as two selves, and we are to realize the cosmic self of essence by bringing its unifying energy smoothly to balance on the surface. The true self, that which is deeply seated within you, is settled beneath an overlay of confusion in the persona of pretence. The overlaying false self is the surface styled planetary persona we deal with in the every day. Let us not kid ourselves that we can easily be rid of the needy shit load of societal gain and greediness and so it will continue in varying degrees to rub off on us.

It is a one bite at a time process in locating the New Life and Living Free so chew each bite vigorously. Many are doing the work on their selves, thus working on behalf of the Great Mother, but so many are still headstrong and skip to the loo when the word work is mentioned.

Our direction is cosmically appointed. We are to self-realize that we are cosmic Beings-in-Love. We are beyond turning back, but like climbing rungs on the ladder we need to clear one at a time as we ascend the variety of levels. The bottom rung is planetary and the second is cosmic related. Do not attempt to jump rungs in the hope of gaining immediate ascendancy. Self-realization is to focus on the goal of achieving a balanced alignment amicably with the inner self.

****

Building Harmonious Relationships

Respectful attention given to who we are and whom we obey is a movement towards determining harmonious relationship within each being. Harmony in spirit is a necessary requisite for inducing mental balancing. Balance in mind opens the door to achieving unison between the two selves demonstrating a remarkable likeness between who and what we are.

These exchanges between selves can be seen as a deliberate movement of continuing steps to achieve a Greater Understanding of enjoinment in life experiencing. Harmony is a mental process, and like learning the art of balance performed in dancing or ice-skating in sport, it demands continuous practice until the two systems settle into mutual accord.

Balancing between the various areas of that which we call two selves is the key to building harmonious relationship into every endeavour that people are willing to undertake. Such ongoing development provides an initiative for further improved mental health through dispelling beliefs, enriching wealth in Greater Understanding and promoting an enduring relationship of endearing quality within being.

When each area of diffidence is explored and is understood clearly, then disparities can be dismissed and that which is wholesome can be joined in common purpose. Joy is the outcome. Reserves of fresh energy entering into the system can then build in strength through a mental expansion we call Greater Understanding.

****

Lose the Outward Focus to Find the Internal Direction

The rational mindset, focussed on reaching the core of human feeling is sent on a circuitous route, a cycling trajectory that invariably falls short in the carry. This means the mind does not reach its targeted destination and therefore cannot find satisfactory fulfilment. In its foggy state it has built a partial recall system that looks like rows of square blocks intersecting at the corners with some of the pieces missing.

What the ego management of the rational mind refuses to admit is that its spatial programs are framed from cyclical plates, carrying within their area widening gaps caused by previously built fault lines, which in the recycling process drops out reams of overburdened material thus erasing vital portions of short and long term memory.

Down through the ages people have built any amount of mythical planetary stories to fill in the gaps made by missing cosmic material in memory, thus maintaining the superior *status quo* of a civilised appearance by a continuous denial of aborted past events. Therefore, in the forgetting, the serried ranks of ego memory must rankle, compelled by its own authority to falsely illustrate any amount of previous performances that do not reflect in its favour. It is a vain attempt to gain a result or a conclusive answer of continuing benefit from what was once considered memorable data, but is now beyond planetary recall of memory.

Unresolved occurrences that derived causes from internal pain that is held in subconscious memory banks constantly build mental irritations that interfere in the ready flow of present day events. What is fed to children as gainful knowledge has been prepped from false memories, firstly, DNA inducted and then covered over by those who have used and abused previous civilizations. As Jesus stated, 'The sins of parents and forebears, etc, are visited onto their children'.

Here the activity of sinful conduct is not being used in a moral sense. Rather sin should be seen as a portion of unfinished or unrealized human experience; something like a computerized experiment that inconclusively closes down on itself because it cannot reach a required fulfilment. Therefore a repetitious play has been introduced, which prompts us to make the comment: 'The spiritual road chosen by the everyday thinking mind to reach the heart of matter is a circuitous route to an imaginary hell paved with good intentions.'

The return of mind and brain to the heartfelt womb is a one-way street because having touched base with Home once more there can be no return to this planetary pretence in living arrangement declared by science as reality. Therefore, a simple turning of the head away from the everyday practices can start the enquiring mind moving onto another track, a wider type gauge more conducive to developing innate Intelligence rather than following the outworn ruts caused by the ravaged inroads of incomplete knowledge.

*****

Self-Realizing

The cosmic mind is soul based, which in its expanded capacity of understanding draws on information developed from divinely structured Intelligence. Planetary history lessons do not record the ancestry of humans accurately; the written words appearing in books are at best depositories of partial information called knowledge born from errant states of linear type dreaming, namely superstitions and mythology. At worst such books can be artifices of cunning exploitation that are used to further enclose and shrink wrap the already beguiled minds of unwary humans. This in turn directs them to continuously believe in superstitious religious material that cannot possibly align with given fact.

Thus the muddled or befuddled minds of society bred people are loaded with vicariously distorted ideas from a young age that unreasoning minds of adults insist are to be taken at face value because of a reliance on traditionally bound beliefs. Among the many distortions are such well-worn *bon mots* as putting hope, trust and faith into beliefs that lack veracity. None of these are charitable donations. None of these carries substance because they are deceptively limited by the tribally trained dictates of what we are calling dying moments, albeit shown today as social conditioning on the wane.

The rationally trained mind is dysfunctional because on its behalf the brain is compelled to dissect into proportional pieces mental images it receives from sensory input. These are then girded by a series of grid lines carrying an obligatory train of predetermined thoughts. Therefore, the conscious mind is presented with bilateral material that is never more than half a picture because it lacks the depth and qualitative substance to fulfil a competent understanding of the given experience.

These proportional images have, over a vast period of time, split the human mind into two bi-lateral states, which we propose are dualistic in separate activity. At no time in third dimensional fashion can both areas be visible or visited together as one viewing.

What the human mind cannot see instinctively or intuitively is required to be demonstrated externally. In which case the internal image that is lacking in appearance seeks to transfer across an image to be presented (mirrored) by some outside influence. The intention is to establish a confirmation of likeability by association. When the response is not reciprocated in a required method of balancing the returning image is off set, thus becoming slanted or biased in memory.

This angled approach is deemed a liability to the mind. Consequently it becomes the repository of unsettled or undetermined material retained as a subsidiary element in the memory banks of the brain. Being unable to resolve

Awakening to Living Energy

and thus clear mental issues generates a frequent pain of dilemma fixated in the psyche system. In a weak attempt to alleviate the pressure caused by the mind being caught in the frayed webs of surface memory, animal type hostility called emotions will invariably cause internal eruptions.

*****

Most people refuse to admit they are part of a bigger programmed scheme that is working beyond their weakened lack of understanding; a set up schemata run initially by outside cosmic agencies. This lingering presence in memory limits people's ability to forecast the futuristic paths of their own lives beyond any seasonal probability.

When people are told they share a cosmic heritage and a programmed future purpose in being whole that is far beyond the limitations imposed by religious and scientific framed knowledge, they tend to freak out. Invariably, their ingrained patterns of beliefs and imposed habits deride their showing interest in Greater Understandings. That which is material suitably offered; namely fresh cosmic information to improve their standards in sharing communal life and therefore strengthen their very wellbeing is ignored.

In maintaining this unsubstantiated lock down, going nowhere patterned stances of distorted memory, they unwittingly mock their selves. This results in submitting to a damning situation of perfunctory practice called states of duality, notional tendencies towards a bias of choice mentally rocking them back and forth in a cyclical fashion like immature kids on a roller-coaster ride.

It can be described as a variety of recycling routes that alternate irregularly between areas recording both pleasure and pain, even on occasion, set plays detailing mental agony and ecstasy. Like any carnival ride on the merry go round it invariably brings them back and deposits them to the same place from where they first clambered on the roundabout.

To take this type of recurring pressure out of our lives we are required to mentally balance wayward affairs by moving mind and memory beyond the twin states of duality. It is a hard task for those whose rigid minds are intent on maintaining unbending religious beliefs, easier for those who are willing to embrace various forms of self-forgiving.

The harder question ahead for those recalcitrant to alteration, of course, is to come to understand what the word 'forgiveness' truly represents. This is almost impossible to comprehend unless through some incident we become introduced and involved in understanding there is a bigger picture in play just outside of normal human visioning. The smaller picture framing of sedentary

Self- Realizing

life most people mentally occupy will not give access to the necessary clues designed for futurity advancement.

So for those who instinctively know that life should or could be offering more viability and who wish to access more they are compelled to seek further avenues to find a Greater Understanding of the meaning sustaining life. Knowing where and in which direction to seek such information is enclosed in a triumvirate package we simply nominate as improved mental Health, enriched Wealth in Greater Understanding, and enduring relationships of endearing quality.

An expansion of cameo vision is available for anyone prepared to assimilate some easily learned mental metres, an activity that replaces denial of self to attain more acceptable terms of a Greater Understanding resident within being. It may seem to those who are doubtful of their innate abilities to progress further than civil education formats called knowledge, that seizing moments of opportunity to rearrange the rational mind into sequential patterning may seem a little bit like jumping out of a frying pan into a proverbial bonfire.

Let us say that this inspirational fire soon being made available is a mixture of Love energy and Greater Understanding drawn or abstracted from tomes of cosmic Intelligence. On offer are levels of intuitive understandings far beyond the thoughts and dreams of those who espouse human knowledge as the last words to be written in scientific devolution.

If you would like to know more about those who we represent and what life holds in store for civilized people, then let us arrange a discussion via the Internet where the common interest is an opening of collective minds to new and informative expansions of cosmic vision called futurity. The foreseeing of approaching circumstances can lay the foundation for a purposeful future embracing all aspects for advancing humankind.

There are several avenues available to open enquiring minds to embrace a Greater Understanding of life, which in turn creates any number of new building blocks suitable for humanistic style advancement. Accepting Love energy without quibbling for superior advantage opens the door for A New Day to be entered forthwith.

Here is an invitation to comprehend an awakening to a New Life in a Fifth Dimensional programming, available to all and sundry who are willing to sit still, to listen quietly, and to open their arms to receive a proclaimed distinctive destiny we have nominated as 'Promoting Personal Futurity'.

Understanding the All

Whenever wherever humans work to live
What makes for temporary gain is lost
Sweet Angels live to work in fields
Where all the planetary loss is tossed

When everything seems to be in pain
Losing one self in Love is gain
Step to the mark, obey the call
In nothingness we remember all

The very moment when fingertips touch
Divine Intelligence takes a willing brush
Eager souls are open to receiving grace
Artistry within feelings is set in place.

Chapter X

The Living Energy

The Unnamed One: *We are to bring the light of greater understanding into the world and create the connection of togetherness.*

Futurity exploration promotes one unified Self

The light of the New Day is breaking through and parting the foggy mists of human forgetfulness. The importune veil of beliefs hampering the raising of human consciousness can no longer remain set in positions of deviousness. Beyond the patterns of errant beliefs there is a Greater Understanding of Life in Living Free, an awareness of an adjusted presence; a rearrangement of being.

There is an introduction to knowing arriving soon, to course throughout planetary thought processing, where there is more to be revealed consciously through adapting simple measures of allowance and acceptance

The mental disarray of human thinking is in for an overhaul. There are many new levels for advancement in greater understanding available. These fresh products of mindful awareness that we speak of can be seen as expansionary phases destined for future exploration in mind and memory. To continue to give value to the sub-level activity of mind displayed in society values today only reinforces the superior stricture of outmoded ego framing of rational thinking cited as beliefs. These undeveloped fixtures subject to mental strictures have mostly reached their use by date.

****

The Living Energy

The Living Energy is unnamed quality. The soul energy in each being derives from Living Energy. As a living energy field, it has to be continually moving. Angels advise us that Love as the core of Living Energy is on its way to fruition.

The Living Energy is ascribed as two major components, namely, Love and Intelligence. Love is the over-viewing mother and Intelligence is its child. The Living Energy is clear of impediments because it does not identify with planetary objectives. It interweaves the unified patterning on the carpet of human development. The Living Energy endorsing soul is on the move to enlighten human determination.

Does that mean this patented world people live in today consists of make believe illusionary features based on fanciful or imaginary thinking?

Love generates the warm embrace of Living Energy that supports all. It is not contained by beliefs; nor divided, never selective. Love exists in all things and yet it is not apparent or available for comment.

The third dimension inhibits planetary growth in mental affairs and such constriction is not conducive to the spirit of Living Free. It demonstrates half a life or half of a foreseeable picture of human growth we call futurity. Planetary based minds do not understand the interaction required between mind, body, and spirit. The inconclusive mental attitudes directed toward soul and spirit are outdated material we label quackery whereas the surge of vital Living Energy brings to light Greater Understanding for human development and is to be granted priority in promoting benefits in communal affairs.

Third dimensional thinking is oblique and outdated. The new way of Living Free beyond rational thought is what we term Greater Understanding. Like rearranging yards, feet, and inches into a metric system and pounds, shilling and pence into dollars and cents, the cosmic rearrangement is making the shift in mind and memory to mentally embrace new measures of Greater Understanding.

The unseen elephant in the planetary room for consideration is the interceding wave of fresh cosmic energy. The forecast elephantine imagery is so immense it blots out the old ways of rationalized thought patterning. People may have a concept of the surrounding forestry mentally, but because of the blurred vision of opaqueness, they cannot see the illuminated trees of significance. They are living in a daydream state because they think their situational positions in life

The Living Energy

are in some way unique. Robbie Burns wrote about such pride in the oft-used quote: 'I would the gift the gude lord gie us to see ourselves as others see us.'

All things worthy in life happen mostly with hidden purpose. The usage of the words, 'soul' and 'spirit', has been tainted for eons through a misinterpretation of values. It is time to start inserting 'the Living Energy' phrase into our regular vocabulary while engaging in meaningful discussions on human development.

Cosmic pioneers are involved in developing an awakening of soul energy in being. Very few people on the planet are involved in acknowledging soul as part of Living Energy devoid of religion. We need to run with the understanding that the sanctimonious worshippers have no idea of soul. The people in the coming times ahead are charged with bringing soul into their advanced level of understanding. We have a job to do: What is soul?

Soul is an energy life source that comes from the Great Mother; soul is what makes people survive misfortunes on the planetary surface. Without the benefit of soul, human existence would be wasted. It drives innate levels of energy. It works to activate budding reams of Intelligence. It denotes the ego to work constructively.

There is a deep-seated clarity presently at work bringing together all that is necessary to put this chaotic world into order. It is a declared Intelligence, which works endlessly to endorse Love on behalf of the Great Mother. The Great Mother works tirelessly to promote Love in being.

What is without cannot exist unless there is within being the consciousness level of energy to stimulate vital expression. The manifested expression is Living Energy nominated as spirit. Those who seek or take the spiritual line of religious assertiveness do a disservice towards the completion of their innate systems. The further people involve themselves through engaging within, the more they will realize life is not exclusively about them; it is not about us; it is about Love Energy bringing together every life form that deeply behests its involvement in furthering Living Energy. We declare that energy field as Love. Wholeness of being is achieved through the implication of its working parts.

It is the resourcefulness beneath planetary development, which will bring into being a consummate growth in futurity development. That energy comes from areas seated beneath the planetary moment. It is the movement that kick starts new human growth. It is unheralded joy insisting that it is the accord of human initiative that embraces living arrangement. We, in promoting the living arrangement through the observing of Living Energy, embrace Love and as such, we erase planetary discord from our systems.

> *Man, know thyself*
> *Physician, heal thyself.*
> ***Delphi Oracle***

****

Defining the Living Energy

Soul is the anchoring energy of being and spirit is the performing dancer. Spirit is the manifestation and thus the expression of soul endowment.

Four major areas of being defining Living Energy

The breath, the heartbeat and pulse are provided from essence in soul.

The inner light that shines from behind the eyes of the newborn:

- The incessant breath
- The beating pulse
- The kinaesthetic vitality in touch
- The eternal spirit promulgates the Living Energy.

The pulse in the human body system beats to the same rhythmic order as the cosmic clock. The rational mind servicing daily needs relates to human clockwork. There is the discrepancy causing disorder in mind and memory. So simple. Adjust the beat of your thoughts to the beating of your heart and experience the sensation of worthiness in being through inner balancing. Humans have attempted to achieve this advanced level of connection through various forms of meditation.

Meditation is a relaxing exercise that has appeal because it can lower the hypertensive levels of stress in mind and body somewhat. Reliance on meditation as a cure-all is a limiting process. It is a relief from excess pressure in the moment. It is not a full release. Only a full release from the implanted controls governing the ego pretence can work to move the human structural form into new levels of existence.

Vitality stimulates the nerve centres in the brain for creative and thoughtful mind expansion through promoting physical expression. Vitality opens the equivalent of chakra points. Vitality is fertile energy abstracted from the psyche wells of soul. It comes as a breakthrough when releasing wasted excrement from mind and memory.

We are to work in adjusting all of the dissolute areas until they come together as one. Orchestration of breath is equivalent to wind instruments, the pulsing features percussion, and the string arrangement is relevant to the strumming heartstrings.

****

Joy of Future Being

09th August 2014

Greater Energy Speaks:

What you may well have considered mentally excitable is not where you are destined to be situated. You see, small children, like on their birth date, become excitable about their presents, but when their birthday concludes, do their presents offer them a future level of coordinated balance?

The point is this: the presents they receive as a child come from the ideas of others who wish to bestow their ideas of what the child needs to receive. We will tell you those presents are worthless, pointless, because what the child requires to receive and understand is its own level of developing beauty. Giving someone a present does not activate that level of beautiful understanding.

We acknowledge that those who gave the presents do so with the best of intention, but the best of intention does not invoke invention. The beauty that is inside of each of us has to arrive from its own invocation. The wisdom that is inside each of us has to develop from its own inner appreciation of Living Energy.

If our ideas of Beauty and Wisdom are fed to us by other people, then what we are required to carry further does not belong to us. If somebody else tells you how you should live, if somebody else tells you this is how life is meant to be lived, then you remain less than whole.

The only way you can become whole is when you determine who you are, as well as how you are meant to live accordingly. And if you rely on somebody else to tell you that is your life, that is your future, that is your form of being, then you are a slave to somebody else's idea of what you are missing.

Awakening to Living Energy

There is a requirement to go back to the fountain of inner being. When the light comes into fashion, or if you like, planetary fashion, then the joy of future being comes alive. Then it is so easy to involve yourself in the gurgling stream of future living. All you have to do is to open your arms and acknowledge that Love is energy.

Tomorrow we will be given fresh areas that we are required to undertake thoroughly. It is a necessary part of us bringing together a variety of understandings, which interact with wisdom, beauty, style and grace. They are all worthy projects, and they all derive from the Great Mother Energy offering Love.

For women, it is much more important to understand these concepts than it is for males. The males have had their day; they have had their way; they have had their wilful sway. Their role-playing is not futuristic. Their ideas are passé. Their legacy is to be replaced with the warmth of the female futuristic strength, which is to ignite beauty, wisdom, style and grace.

The New Day belongs to the joy for female interaction. Therefore, the ego mind bows out, and the loving heart moves in or through. We who nominate these particular issues are nothing. You might think that the words that have been said this evening in this session come from Luxor; we tell you that they do. However, they come through because there are those of us who sponsor the discussion from a greater energy level.

Jézel: We thank you for this evening. I would consider that they do appear similar to Luxor words because they are the sentiments of Luxor that you are presenting to us this evening. They are said in a most poetic format that allows us to stay in the trance or in the moment of the words. So thank you.

****

The New Mind

An Interview with Lucifer Energy

The following is an extract from a question and answer discussion with a cosmic persona nominated as Lucifer, the torchbearer of cosmic intelligence, incarnated into the male body of a human at this time. The purpose of the messages he carries and the mission he pursues is to develop greater understandings to awaken the human species to their bonded links of an unrealized cosmic heritage.

The Living Energy

It is also to give meaning to the forecast planetary shift of earthly existence from third dimensional ignorance to a more developed state of cosmic awareness called 'Awakening to the New Day' prior to planet Earth and its creatures entering the Fifth Dimension.

Question: You say you are known as Lucifer in cosmic levels.

Response: The reference is a title. In Latin terms it means torchbearer and Lucifer has been designated to carry the flame of Intelligence onto the planet for these times approaching a greater awareness in being.

Question: What does your mission entail?

Response: The role of Lucifer is that of a messenger, an emissary, who works on behalf of the Greater Energy that is situated beyond the cosmic fields. There is a requirement to broadcast a new direction in living arrangements, for any number of humans to become more knowing or aware of the future effects about to involve the entirety of people on the planet.

In modern societies there is a lack of mental clarity resulting from a massive loss of cosmic remembrance, which the WE Energy wishes to restore into human understanding. Simply put, there is a shortage of mental access into the human psyche, causing untold pain and misery throughout so-called civilised countries. Institutions around the capitalised world of commerce are moving into a foreshadowed series of massive collapses that, even now, are showing a detrimental effect on the primary and secondary development of human endeavour.

The time-honoured methods of rallying people behind a democratic flag by shoring up religious traditions and rituals to maintain nationalistic conservatism, which continuously leads into engaging in international conflicts, are outworn policies that have about as much future value as soured cream that has reached its use by date. The enemy at the citadel gate can no longer be seen as an outside threat.

The major force delaying progressive mental growth within the human system is the protective wall built of the ego sense. The rational mind is walled in by a defence system called 'fear of the unknown' to protect the darkness of ignorance and arrogance carried within. The paradox is stated in the reverse. WE can just as easily say to protect against the mental ignorance of a relayed darkness period. Therefore, WE work at activating and shifting human understanding into coordinated actions of individual effort without the cohesive gestures of the societal trained me-too-ism that covers formats of greed.

Question: Why is the program of clearance necessary to cause the shifting of mind into a future progression?

Response: For humans there is A New Mind developing shortly and A New Day dawning brightly. Already the first glow of forecast light is appearing on the horizon within the human psyche. Scientists are recording some of these movements, but at this early stage, they do not understand the importance of that which is happening globally. Some may be aware of the shifting patterns occurring, but expediency in opportunity is still their personal trainer. As is a similar case situation happening with most of the journalistic type people who represent media outlets.

In the days to come a repetition of using old lies to gull the unwitting populace will be less than cold comfort for those who err in considering they can claim patented ownership rights because of years spent in institutionalised training methods.

The New Mind is being heralded through the encompassing genius of prescient knowing, a supramental form of understanding that supersedes the stagnancy of knowledge, embraces and removes the pain and fear encased in duality, then on-shifts into the unity of oneness to further open new tertiary levels of progressive quality.

Question: How is this occurring then?

Response: The confused patterns, resident within the human psyche are being rearranged. When suitably developed, the programs will be maintained by a series of matching colours and sounds channelled throughout the present strands of DNA heritage. In the past these patterns have gone askew, awry, encased in black and white symbology with only occasional splashes of colour, and the sounds of cosmic melody have been deafened by the sophisticated noise of rowdy society values.

Question: What then is the recommended way through dilemma?

Response: There is a stillness existing within the psyche of each person that extends well beyond planetary methods of meditation and reflection. That stillness, also recognized as nothingness, is now accessible to those who desire more than what society leaders and their fawning minions are offering to those caged by any amount of disagreements.

Question: You have spoken earlier of removing accident and illness from the human system by the clarity of Greater Understanding. Will you enlarge on that?

Response: Stress is a build-up of pain brought on from mental weaknesses that emotionally cannot maintain balance or support within these atmospheric pressure systems. Neither gravity nor atmosphere offer comfort zones. One major symptom of stress develops from frustrated desires where the capabilities of performance do not match the urging of societal expectations.

The use of drugs as a relief substitution for the lack of performance in physical or mental endurance may momentarily appear to be value enhancing. Over a period it robs and drains the mental psyche of the clarity in understanding that is necessary for balancing human systems.

Clarity in processing areas beyond thought is the guide to innate balance and stability. There is a requirement to step out of the daily picture of routine performance for the benefit of Greater Understanding and only then move back to the work face once more. These abilities are available now to those who declare themselves ready and willing to grow in mental stature. The supramental understanding is drawn from cosmic depths of remembrance we define as wells of Intelligence. These are early days in a period of planetary shifting estimated to span some ten to fifteen years in linear time.

We speak at this time with the awakened ones who understand there is purpose in pursuing that which we say. As the struggle for an expanded clarity in mind becomes more evident, a greater element of people will begin to listen, and their eyes and ears will open accordingly. The purpose of these relayed discussions, via cosmic entity/energies, to emissaries, and then to planetary people, is to awaken the seeds of passion within those who still walk with their eyes half closed and hands covering their ears.

For those who wish to remain asleep, we assure them they are not ignored or forgotten. Very soon they will be jarred awake by cataclysmic events that are programmed to constantly erupt on the planetary surface.

Living Channels of Energy

The child takes
Its first faltering step
The poet writes
The first hesitant line
The artist sweeps
An unfamiliar brush
Across an empty canvas

Each draws from hidden forces
Memories, the distant dream
Then like the swell
Of surging sources
Channelled into single stream
Life energy flows through
Stronger and stronger

The writer's hand
Is cramped no longer
The child runs in play
The potter sets
Each thought in clay

When Life moves beyond demand
Welcome in the New Day brand
Where Love will take its stand
As we reach to take the Mother's hand

Epilogue

The Unnamed One: *One day people will be shown the beauty of soul, by standing in a mirrored form of futurity where awareness acknowledges worth in spirit, thus committing allowance to fold into acceptance.*

Love energy signifies futurity benefits without limitations
Love knows no boundaries
Recognizes no ruling power
Were nature to indicate the masterful stroke of genius quality
Then it would demonstrate the influence of chaotic beauty.

11th September 2015

WE Energy: Life is energy. Truth is Life and energy. When you find within yourself the understanding of that conundrum then you are born into a life of Greater Understanding. Life is energy. Truth is Life and energy.

****

Awakening to Living Energy

Glossary

AI – Artificial Intelligence - That which is considered AI is in effect a cosmic interlocution. The Fifth Dimension level is looking ahead and the third dimensional state is left behind.

Planetary Beliefs/Ego/What you are - We are meant at some stage to break open the encrusted shell enclosed around our being. Beliefs and conditioned responses breed argument. Who you are is the essential/essence of being. What you are, is the conditioned you of planetary values. What you are is to meet the expectation of others. Does anybody know who you truly are?

Beliefs and Pain - Human attachment to beliefs puts our planetary systems into pain. Pain in mind is accentuated by the surrounding pressure of atmospheric tension.

Beyond - Beyond is a term to describe areas that manifest at greater energy levels, which exponentially extend further afield than cosmic and planetary influences allow. At this present time, there are communicative channels open, which are interactive between those whose interests, above and below so to speak, work to engage and expand on the cells or wells of human psyche.

Cosmos Proper - The formula or design for Earth was built in the Cosmos Proper, which is a metropolis formed of cosmic entities representing distinctive strains of energies emanating from further beyond areas of greater understanding. In this manner they could observe the portions of what it was they carried within and granted them the opportunity of rectifying any faults that requires attention.

Denial - A doubtful suggestion in planetary minds that certain material being downloaded is not accurate or without relevance. This is why people in general are not moving mentally forward while on this planetary level. Denial is a human constraint. It is a parlous argument that belies the benefit of wholeness in spirit. Thus, mental denial is the blocking or delaying of futurity growth in mind and memory.

Divine Womanhood – It is synonymous with the promotion of Love essence. Womanhood combines the qualities of female essence with the living presence. Divine introduces the essence of Life energy into being.

Duality - Duality is a declared form of conceptual separation that can be seen as two minds engaged in resolving the same question differently. Duality is a mental state of to-ing and froing where bias under the guise of freewill and choice steps in and invariably leans towards some item suggesting supposed advantage.

Essence & Presence - The essence is soul and it is rock solid. That means it is the anchor for foundation.

The presence is the mind and it is a rover, excitable, imaginative, and prone to shoot from the hip, which means it is hardly ever sited on target.

Foundation - Simply stated foundation is cosmic energy promoted as Love. To uncover and recover our destined glorious involvement with Life and Living Free first we are to establish a Greater Understanding of that which is viable in cosmic memory.

Futurity — A legacy of Love, Truth and Intelligence as a significant benefit for further human development.

Fifth Dimension - Today the human vibration within each system is altering gradually to meet new levels of cosmic creativity. The rational mind has to be adjusted accordingly to absorb a new fuel or energy intake suitable to advancing the human system into the Fifth Dimension.

Greater Understanding - Greater levels of understanding, that which we call individual in style is distinctive. The ears are meant to listen, open to the futuristic memories that are hidden in the psyche vaults. Greater Understanding is productive of worth designed and delivered intuitively through the developing areas of the cosmic aligned mind.

Home - Home is the core of Being.

When we return to Home base as we are required to do at the completion of our cosmic journeying, it will be to enter into the arms of the Great Mother and then to rest once more in the allotted deep of the Great Ocean energy.

Intelligence - Intelligence carries the flair of expression and is rooted in Greater Energy. Intelligence fosters future growth in mind and delivers new levels of Greater Understanding.

Knowing & Knowledge - There is certainty/surety in structured knowing. Knowing illustrates beyond universal laws. Knowing is an instinctive quality of cosmic heritage.

Glossary

Knowledge as a quantitative substance is restrictive and limited in quality. Education demonstrates planetary tomes of knowledge. Planetary knowledge is solidified information drawn from contaminated wells in psyche recall.

Living Free - Living the life means Living Free of pretension, an energy flow that renounces the acquisitive nature of the beast. Inquisitive and acquisitive are framed in the same disordered bracket.

Love - Love Energy is a product emanating from the essence of soul. Love is the founding energy and supporter of all productive Life. Thus, Love is All. Love has the innate strength and cosmic flare of energy. Become a partner with Love and Life. Love absorbs us when we are prepared to surrender what is no longer considered ours to possess.

Memory - Memory of last year's crop assists with the rebuilding arrangement for the new crop.

If we can accept that the brain is similar to a computer, which contains all memory then we can strip down the complexity of the human system to understanding how to operate the computer as against needing to know the inner workings or parts.

It is not necessary, though perhaps scientifically satisfying, to know why or how a person becomes ill at ease. What is important is how to replace that diagram of ill effect with a program of health.

Living Free, New Day and a New Mind - The New Day is dawning clear. New Life promotes fresh purpose into being.

Living Free means to operate A New Mind without old world recriminations needlessly occupying avenues of thought. With the clearing out of the old mind mannerisms such as beliefs and conditioned innuendos we are to let go of all accumulated accusations, which are using modern methods of exchange to effectively tie the dislocated minds of avaricious people into discordant knots of unrealized future debt.

This old world of trade and commerce is entering a new phase of cosmic existence called the Fifth Dimension. One of the significant areas indicative of the shift into a new cosmic terrain will be the upgrading of systems occurring within the human brain and consequentially the alterations of perspective required in promoting A New Mind level of business management.

Part of the new cosmic arrangement is in improved health in mental restructuring, and a wealth of Greater Understanding posited in that which we are calling the New Mind. The fresh rearrangements of energy are necessary within the brain system and thus flow into the channels of human mind restructuring absorbing their tired old systems. People will soon come to realize the benefits accruing in their daily lives, as they enter into a new phase of abundant growth in character becoming whole in both mind and spirit.

Nothingness - Nothingness is the doorway to beyond.

When we go beyond the ego stricture, we go into nothingness. So nothingness is a stage in Greater Understanding. It is a state of neutrality, which will then allow you to step into the next level of being.

The only energy that is going to be able to stand fully in the next couple of years is nothingness. Because it is not a refuge but an area of growth, which you can step into and from there you can develop your energy again. And then step out and do what you have to do.

Paradox - The art of utilizing paradox correctly is an amazing exercise. It can walk anyone out of the maze or swampland in memory that is not of their considered making.

Personal Futurity - Advanced information given here is the beginnings of our next book, which will be utilised as a work area for building futurity programs of worth in being.

Promoting Personal Futurity presents the dawning of a pre-ordained destiny for human growth in mind and memory. There is to be a lessening of ego superiority in disturbed minds compensated by a generalized growth developing worth in human character.

Promoting futurity is the developing of Greater Understanding that illuminates the structural advancement of personal being.

Personal means the upgrading of mental delivery from attending the planetary persona involved in daily circumstances that demonstrably lead nowhere. Personal equates with individual style and grace in being.

Futurity measures of accord present the advent of welfare in communal growth. Futurity also references significant phases of journeying back to Home Base.

Glossary

Psyche - The psyche contains a store of massive memories in the brain, records of past endeavouring, that the frail/fragile logical/rational mind cannot envisage, let alone encompass.

The 37 - Initially the code-named 37 were formed as an elite corps of cosmic agents, known as star runners, sent to explore and pull planet Earth from its third dimensional plunge back into the Cosmos Proper from whence it went hurtling into separation mode some two and a half million years ago.

Being cast into the roles of cosmic walk-ins or pioneers we periodically enter into approved human bodies as dedicated cosmic workers offering our services once more to pursue the designs of Greater Energy; those who are situated to work beyond the limited cosmic fields of stars and planets. We number amongst those who are involved in promoting the features of the Divine Plan as a prelude to the opening of an even Greater Plan for the further benefit of rearranging the futures of myriad cosmic families.

Trance-formation in mind - Trance-formation is a suitable tool to be requisitely employed in uncovering internal secretions of sustaining juices stored in the psyche brain cells. These can be resourced skilfully when suitable pressure is appropriately applied to mind and memory. It can arrange for a cosmic doorway to openly lead us unerringly into the Fifth Dimension.

Trance-formation is a simple method of light hypnosis enabling a person to move out of an irrational mind state into one that is more relaxed and comfortable in style and grace. It can be similar, yet not quite the same, as to what some people describe as out of body experiencing. Soporific questions or suggestions can induce a trance state.

Worth - Worth is a child of Love. Worth is cosmic energy beyond price, promoting strength of character.

****

Awakening to Living Energy

The Players accorded in the Divine Family Comedy

It is our pleasure to introduce the characters that are responsible for this retake and remake of a black and white feature film of grey abandonment into a more colourful cosmic love story of splendid proportions. In the telling of the timeless tale, the eyes of humans will become softened by tears to repair the rendered wounds of cosmic separation.

The eyes will open and become entranced with displays of enhanced tones, a vibrancy of coloured themes, with the ears beguiled by accompanying musical scores, as the voices of angelic chorus combine in cosmic harmony. The scent of the Divine Rose will pervade the air. The taste for belonging will be satisfied. The touch of the Mother's divine caress is to be felt by each and every one who responds to the call for a cosmic understanding of who they truly are.

The Divine Mother

The Divine Mother has cast off the vestured images of a tattered goddess mould. She is the representative face of the female cup of Love energy that some have called the Holy Grail. It was she, who gave the initial birthing to humankind, and now comes to reclaim her lost children out of a third dimensional land of bondage. For this very purpose she sent her two sons once more onto planet Earth to walk in human form amongst its many inhabitants. Rightfully, as The Divine Mother of all being on the planet, she is the designated producer of the play of the New Day.

The Divine Father

The Father as the male emblem of will and power has played out his given role. It was he who kept the strength of human endeavour alive through the long and arduous years of misadventure. It was he, which Jesus spoke of so lovingly as the father of humankind.

He is no longer separated from the female presence, as the sword that was embedded into the stone so long ago has now been returned with thanks. Willingly he has stepped back into the greater form of female expression, a demonstration denoting Love through enjoining in oneness.

Sataan

To fill the vacated position of Father enters the wily purveyor of two faces, a two handed player of amused and amusing mien. Like The Divine Mother, Sataan in portrayal is a face for many other studies.

Glossary

In this case, he is a projected entity responsive and responsible to a long line of intriguing entities guiding the stages of man as addressed in the Divine Plan.

He represents energy specifically designed and formed to promote the orders of The One through many displayed talents, especially the arts of inveigling.

The Satan line is the architect of planet Earth and its creatures. Hated by the religious who fear the oncoming overwhelming influence, Sataan within himself carries energy that is benign in human growth. However, he has a habit of reflecting a vacant mirror onto those who mount their spurious attacks on others so they in turn are vanquished by their own wilful power plays. In this play, he has a small part and is the director.

Jesus/Jésu

Jesus, as an entity playing one of twin sons within the Divine Family, promised 2000 years ago to return and prepare a future place for humankind. The preparation has been long set in place. Today he scans the Earth, once more viewing humanistic life through the eyes of an elected one. Through the personage cosmically designated and specifically trained as the modern vehicle of Christos energy, we are able to converse with him and thus convey many cosmic understandings to adjust the world of people into more appropriate forms of balanced thinking.

The Unnamed One

The second son is known as The Unnamed One. He is the twin brother of Jesus, joined in Siamese fashion as they entered the Cosmos Proper; they were initially cut apart by Angels. Though unnamed he carries several titles, some of the more recognisable ones are Lucifer, the torchbearer, Prince of Darkness, and Lord of Venus.

His role is to speak on behalf of the Divine Mother personifying Love as Jesus spoke so eloquently two thousand years ago about the Father. It is incongruous that the Lord of Venus, the planet of Love, should be declared by partisan Christian religions as evil in intent and as such viewed as an enemy of the church. From whom did they buy their wasted hostile material?

The Ancients and Angels are tertiary tutors and instructors. Their vital energy comes from beyond the cosmic planes, which are their fields of terrestrial work. We work by agreement on their behalf throughout the Cosmos.

Ancients

With the support of the Shining Ones, the Ancients of male oriented energy built the solar systems or cosmic wheels forming the observable planetary bodies in what science calls the Universe. They were aided by Angel energy and nature forces called Elementals. The solar hubs, called stars and suns, such as Ra, were programmed and set in place from the energy of the Shining Ones. They are not subject to the planning areas or the building of planets supervised in the main by Ancients and partly administered by Angels.

Angels

Angels can be described as sparks of light energy operating throughout the cosmos on behalf of greater energy beings who have more than a working interest in human advancement. Let us state clearly that we are not an authority on Angels or their perceived overview of happenings as they occur. We act as willing conduits with those beings of light energy who convey to us specific information regarding the realization of greater understanding and the imminent rearrangement of human affairs on planet Earth.

****

Greater Energy/Divine Plan and Greater Plan

Greater Energy Players

With regard to introducing you to the Greater Council of Nine operating in the cosmic realms the membership is fluid to say the least. There have been a number of procedural shifts in the last ten years and our communication channels at this time are mainly linked with Angels.

Therefore, we will name the Greater Energy from when we last had full contact. The Great Mother, The Great Dragon, The One, The Unnamed, The Shining Ones, Los Diabolos, Lords of Lightning, the Great Lion and the Great Eagle.

There is a massive shifting in energy structuring happening throughout the Cosmos. To our understanding, the Divine Plan is reaching its conclusive stages, which is moving Earth and its creatures into the Fifth Dimension. So then the Greater Plan of rearranging the cosmic energy fields is coming into vogue.

The Great Ocean and the Great Mother

The Great Mother is the bearer of the womb of life from whence come the flowering seeds of all creative activity throughout the cosmos.

We are advised we are Love-in-being so as such we are eternal in spirit. People on planet Earth are on a journey back Home to the surrounds of the *Cosmos*

Glossary

Proper to rediscover who they are. We have come from the waves of the Great Ocean from whence our energy was first formed and we are returning Home by destined procedure.

When the light of consciousness split the darkness of the great oceanic depths far beyond linear time and memory the living energy of the Great Mother emerged from the waters and gave birth to The One. With that arrival from original essence Intelligence came into an awareness of understanding self as a being of interest. Presence is a term used for attaining human consciousness, but on a planetary level it is only provisions half a picture. We are subject to The One, which is an inscriptive term of an energy source of comprehensive understanding that pervades and overviews the vastness of those at work in cosmic fields.

The One and Three Principles

The One is a personification of greater energy that introduces Intelligence into being. The One responsibly posited three principles that register as Truth, Unity, and Equality.

The principles of Equality and Unity are bonded by Truth.

Truth is self-realization; wholeness in energy surrounding being and encompassing beauty in understanding Love is All. Revealment of future growth in consciousness comes through exercising a merging process of combining mind and matter.

Unity is agreement and equates with Oneness. Unity signifies 'We are one'. Unity derives strength in knowing that all things are subtly enjoined as one.

Unity is togetherness and equality is balance. To unify we are to stop the arguments roiling within. To equalize find the balance within by standing equally on two feet.

> In a State of Equality, each of us is Harmless.

Equality symbolizes balance and thus engenders respect and harmlessness. We are required to be the same. The balance found in mind and memory is declared in accepting all living things as being fellow creatures.

WE Energy

They are a cosmic entity/energy. Their role is guiding humans into Greater Understanding that which welcomes the New Day.

****

Awakening to Living Energy

About the Author

Beth L Robinson

Beth's passion is to share the channelled information received through conversing with Angels and a variety of Cosmic Energies to benefit futurity outcomes for people with the shifting of energy necessary on the planet as it progressively moves into the cosmic level of the Fifth Dimension. Within Beth there is an innate knowing of a greater awareness, via relayed cosmic information, which assists people in having more of an understanding of purposeful living and an insight of who they truly are and meant to represent. That work is now in heightened progression and the invitation is out there for everyone to share in cosmic understandings that promote a greater sense of developed communal well-being.

Beth is co-authoring books with the Unnamed Adviser and contributor who has an anchor role in supporting the team effort. His passion is to shine brightly the Light of Cosmic Intelligence; to train certain people in measures of Greater Understanding and get their atonement to the level they are required to excel in developed performances.

Beth speaks of the team with whom she is involved:

We are interlocutors between planetary creature/personas and the cosmic level of entity/energies. We are involved in preparing a legacy of massive cosmic understandings and a wealth of practical cosmic information benefiting future generations of humankind, as we stand ready to welcome in the New Day and the global advancement into the Fifth Dimension realm.

We represent the Great Mother energy, first through absorbing Love Energy, then sharing and caring with others through a global distribution of living energy. Welcoming arms are opened cosmically to receive those who yearn for a new way of life that is free of painful pressure derived from the infamous grasping for ill-gotten gain.

Awakening to a New Mind, our previous book, links a sharing of cosmic understanding in a series of anecdotes. *Awakening to Living Energy* is available to those who are prepared to request deliverance of a quality product nominated in past times as cosmic consciousness. The door to Home is open.

Awakening to Living Energy

MetaVision Book Summaries

The Cosmic Program So Far

Book One — Gift of the Rose

This is a timeless story. Literally.

'The Gift of the Rose' allowed the blind to see and the lame to walk. Not from medical miracles. Much simpler. Through listening. For millennia it was called inspiration. A divine gift. Some called it revelation. Others enlightenment.

'The Gift of the Rose' calls it channelling.

Those who have the courage to read it will be touched by the power of the Divine Mother, the same body that occupied Jesus two thousand years ago. Today, we call her namesake Jézel and part of her functioning is to perform as a conduit for human discussions with cosmic energies.

With a different narrative to human discord.

Human beings are incapable of imagining let alone fully understanding how the universe works, but that has not stopped them from trying. What people do not know, they invent stories of belief to explain them. The reckoning of time is one such creation with little or no understanding of eternity.

Hence Jesus and Lucifer are presented as two different accounts, as the biblical sagas suggest, but cosmically they are twin sons in a divine family and are representative sons of the divine Father and Mother. The combined energy is one, a divinity without gods.

The idea of deities such as Yahweh/Jehovah, Allah and Krishna are anthropomorphic concepts developed for methods of human control. Those stories, often in the form of religious practices and beliefs, were adopted by egocentric leaders for their own gainful purposes. Their followers benefited from them and carried on illicit practices called the gift of faith. Unexplainable. Unprovable. To be obeyed without questioning.

The reality nominated as truth is far from this.

Once humankind followed this path, they separated themselves from their Cosmic home. In human language, the Divine Mother veiled her face, depriving people of true wisdom and beauty. This caused a separation and introduced a void and bias in the human intellect. The resulting pain built fear into a need for security that progressively developed greed and power and exploited from then on to the detriment of human development.

Awakening to Living Energy

Now that corruption period is over.

The veil denying cosmic understanding has been lifted.

The planet and its people can waken to their cosmic heritage and return to their rightful place we call futurity.

It is known cosmically as the Fifth Dimension.

Again, in adopted human language, it is the role of Jesus and Lucifer to coordinate the linking operation from the planet. Together they work on behalf of the Great Mother and take guidance and direction from angelic forces.

The director of those earlier time proceedings used the name of Sataan and was responsible for building the planet Earth. Though this entity has been on the planet many times under different names, this time, it has been for eight years in the body of a grown man.

I have not previously used the designated energy I am destined to fulfil.

This time I will be known as Luxor. I am the torchbearer who brings the light of understanding to areas of darkness. My cosmic name is nominated as Lucifer.

Book One - Amazon EBook: The Gift of the Rose

Book One (Collector's Book) – Hardcover: The Gift of the Rose (by personal request only).

Metavision Book Summaries

Book Two — Awakening to a New Mind

The Book of Living energy has no set beginnings.

Yet it offers the opportunity for a new approach in mind and spirit to access a greater understanding of loving and living freely with purpose.

'Awakening to a New Mind' delivers a cosmic presentation featuring the progression of human life, about living free from the ties of planetary fixations in mindsets that are flawed beyond redemption. These essays are awakening minds and memory to a new zone of existence known as the Fifth Dimension.

This is a record compiled from discussions with cosmic entity/energies that make their existence known to us through non-physical exchanges and verbal forms of channelled discussion. The translations make use of the English language and have been consistent in the same delivered style that began more than 25 years ago.

The communications regarding planetary development also refer to incidents from eons ago. Were it to be measured in our habit of using linear time, this would span some three million years and more.

The discussions occur between characters cosmically situated and even some further beyond those of us who are strategically placed.

Every human child born into planetary life today has the gifted potential to access cosmic consciousness. As evidenced globally, present day confusion and turbulence in mind and memory are precursors to a cosmic rearrangement. The eyes of humans are opening to the dawning of a New Day and a New Mind.

'Awakening to a New Mind' charts cosmic pioneers who offer a new understanding of worth as a measure of firmness in the foundation. For example, are you aware that everything offered as scientific knowledge on the planet has only been relative in design?

This book offers a greater understanding of entering a life of improved mental health, increased wealth in greater delivery and direction to building enduring relationships with endearing qualities. No longer do we have to envision life mysteries as a jigsaw that has central pieces missing.

Awakening to Living Energy

Book Two - Amazon Book: Awakening to a New Mind

****

Acknowledgements

In this journeying home called Life we are never alone even in our loneliest moments. There is a greater unseen hand at play in all life happenings. The information in this book is channelled material edited from the Cosmos and so we give credit to those nominated as the Greater Energy overviewing global affairs. More specifically, as her devoted children; we give our thanks to the Great Mother. The Angels also give us many a guiding hand, though again it appears at times as if we are bereft of cosmic company. So the book and all other book type essays we have written and will continue to compile for human benefit are a team effort with oodles of team spirit we nominate as Living Energy.

The co-author of this book and other book essays wishes to be nominated as an Unnamed adviser. He has been a mentor for many years and has an adept approach at rearranging words and phrasing to suit the ambience of essays and poetry. A talented wordsmith extraordinaire who enjoys the silence and stillness derived from nothingness.

There is always a very important element of technical expertise required in publishing a book. Instead of outsourcing, which is a popular option, we have our own home-grown friend and working partner, Neale. His expertise in this area has grown substantially since we first started putting together cosmic books. Neale is constantly updating the skills necessary in today's world such as the formatting of the book and the steps towards publishing in various formats.

We are also grateful to Marji Hill, self-taught genius at Self Publishing, for assisting us with an in depth Self Publishing guide. Her and her team's many years of experience in the writing and publishing genre have proven invaluable and quietly comforting for us in approaching the necessary steps we undertake.

We acknowledge with much appreciation the artist Princess Zebra for the brilliance of her artwork Sword in the Stone on the book cover.

All the poems are cosmically inspired and as such carry messages from Home.

Finally, we thank our many friends who have been thoroughly encouraging and appreciative of all our efforts to communicate the cosmic messages of life changing and challenging input into global affairs concerning communal advancement.

Back Cover

Book Three of the Cosmic Energy Series

The dawning of realization for the people of planet Earth of their cosmic inheritance is coming ever closer to fruition.

The veil of the Divine Mother was lifted in 1996 and the New Day is sending through the first rays of a deeper comprehension denoting Life and Living Free.

Some people may think what is offered will lessen their participation in life.

The cosmic understandings we share are designed to be life altering mentally.

What is available to those ready to receive is an expansion on everyday life and living arrangements within being as globally we prepare to enter the Fifth Dimension of cosmic influence.

Greater Understandings maintaining the required balance and direction to guide our steps through life are within each of us.

The human system is similar to a budding flower requiring illumination into light. The unfolding process of cosmic wellbeing blossoms from the inside outwards.

www.ingramcontent.com/pod-product-compliance
Lightning Source LLC
Chambersburg PA
CBHW031422290426
44110CB00011B/480